AMERICAN EVANGELICALISM

AMERICAN EVANGELICALISM

Conservative Religion and the Quandary of Modernity

JAMES DAVISON HUNTER

Rutgers University Press

New Brunswick, New Jersey

Library of Congress Cataloging in Publication Data

Hunter, James Davison, 1955–
American evangelicalism.

Bibliography: p.
Includes index.
1. Evangelicalism—United States—History—20th century.
2. United States—Church history—20th century.
I. Title.
BR1642.U5H86   277.3'082   82–317
ISBN 0–8135–0960–2   AACR2
ISBN 0–8135–0985–8 (pbk.)

To Honey

Contents

Tables

Preface

This book is both for those on the outside who would like to look in at the Evangelical world and for those Evangelicals on the inside who are interested in understanding themselves better. As much as this book is about American Evangelicalism, it is also about modernity, the modernization process, and how people cope in this unprecedented period in history. Thus I hope it will attract the attention of those concerned with the effects of modernity on all people and all world views. I especially hope it will reach those who find it difficult to reconcile their heritage and present convictions with the constraints built into modernity.

Naturally, my efforts in researching and writing this book were not unaided. The editorial staff of *Christianity Today* and in particular Paul Robbins must be thanked for granting the use of their data. The Princeton Religious Research Center, the organization responsible for collecting the survey data, must also be acknowledged for the technical assistance involved in making the data physically available to me. In working through the substantive concerns of this research, I was assisted more than once by conversations with Paul Collins, Stephen Ainlay, Joseph Foreman, Marvin Waterstone, Don Dayton, Harry Bredemier, and Ben Zablocki. I am grateful to Robert Wuthnow, who proved to be a reliable source of methodological and theoretical insight as well as a source of good counsel, and to Peter Berger for his predictably cogent comments on early drafts of the manuscript. For moral support of the most enduring sort, I am indebted to my parents, Robert and LaRue Hunter. Finally, I owe my most profound gratitude to my wife, Helen Stehlin Hunter, to whom this book is dedicated—a modest and entirely inadequate recompense for her able and tireless editorial and technical assistance as well as her sustaining companionship while the book was being written.

Part One

THEORETICAL CONSIDERATIONS

1

Definitions and Perspectives

When the word *Evangelical* comes up in conversation today, a variety of stereotypes are usually evoked. One is the canary-throated evangelist in an orange double-knit leisure suit, puce-colored socks, and white "Pat Boone" loafers, and his wife in a knee-length chiffon dress, tan-shaded hose, white medium-height heels, and a beehive hairdo, standing before a congregation of like-costumed brethren and assuring them, with Cheshire grins, that the blessing of the Lord will soon descend upon them. Another is the conservative Republican politico attired in a three-piece suit from J. C. Penney, his countenance one of good-humored "Christian" affability, yet his heart the embodiment of rigid moral and political dogma. Often linked with these images are such adjectives as "anti-intellectual," "socially uncouth," and "morally immature." Although stereotypes often do have some grounding in truth, they are always to some degree a distortion. When they gain wide currency in the culture, they prejudice fair discussion and truncate open-minded and in-depth analysis. This has certainly been the case for the Evangelicals and their movement. Evangelicalism has for too long failed to receive open-minded treatment.

One important reason for the wide dependence on caricatures in the discussions of Evangelicalism is the regrettable lack of social-scientific literature on the phenomenon, for research would undoubtedly clarify and qualify, if not contradict, our current understandings. When one hears in the popular media that Evangelicals constitute between one-fifth and one-third of the American population, one would naturally suppose that there would be a body of substantial knowledge about so large a group. In fact we know far less than what we purport to know. The stereotypes are comfortable and ostensibly reliable. Among the reasons cited for this lack of research are the political and social-class biases of many researchers against what they consider intrinsically lower class, politically conservative, and historically nonprogressive (Warner, 1979). Whatever the reasons, two questions await a more careful response: Who are they? and What are they engaged in?

3

The mere existence of such large numbers of conservative Protestants in contemporary America presents a mystery. It is a commonplace among the sophisticated and the barely literate alike that "being religious is not as easy as it used to be"—a phenomenon social scientists call *secularization*. There is something about modernity that erodes the plausibility of religious belief and weakens the influence of religious symbols in the social structure and culture at large. The query is simply this: if modernization secularizes and America is among the most modern societies in the world, how then is it possible that Evangelicalism survives and even thrives in contemporary America? The relationship between modernity and Evangelicalism is peculiar for another reason as well. It is a widely held view that Protestantism was at least partially responsible for spawning the modernization process in the West (Weber, 1958), prompting the questions: What has happened to ascetic Protestantism during the past century in America? Has it remained constant or has it been changed by those same structures and symbols it initially helped to create? If it has changed, why and how?

In the following chapters I attempt to answer these questions through empirical examination of the ways this religious movement and its world view have interacted and do interact in a dialectic with the institutional structures and processes of modernity. This entails examining the ways Evangelicalism accommodates, resists, and legitimates the forces of modernity. First I must briefly explain the meaning of the central concepts of this book, *modernity* and *contemporary American Evangelicalism*, for each is fraught with a measure of ambiguity and surrounded with its own history of controversy.

Modernity

In the analysis of modern society, a number of theoretical models have emerged. Two of the most prominent are the development paradigm and the classical paradigm; the former has been the dominant research framework. The development paradigm has largely been applied to studies of the dynamics of the modernization process in the social systems of non-Western societies, that is, the specific forces behind social, economic, and political growth of particular "underdeveloped" or "developing" societies.[1] In most cases the research objective has been to uncover the key operative modernizing forces as they interact within a specific historical tradition. More precisely, the objective has been to explore the nature of the processes at work in the transition from underdeveloped to developed societies and the possible variations in such a transition.

The surge of "development" literature has loosely corresponded with the general interest government and the private sector have taken in the so-called Third World and the "new states." As a result of major funding by government and industry, the underlying focus of interest of much of this research has been political: how it is possible to develop the underdeveloped societies and what shape foreign policy should take given the stage of development of a particular society. The political left has been critical of this alliance to the point of dubbing the resulting literature a scientific ideology of imperialism (Bodenheimer, 1968).

Research in modernization has been so oriented by the development paradigm that the term *modernization* is often considered synonymous with development. Actually, this perspective is a relatively new one based on the repudiation of the "inadequacies" of the classical paradigm, which goes back to the social philosophers of the classical period of sociology. Central to the classical paradigm is a qualitative typological distinction between premodern, traditional, or gemeinschaft societies and modern, industrial, or gesellschaft societies.[2] Irrespective of important social, economic, political, and cultural differences between societies, all premodern societies have significant common characteristics that distinguish them from modern ones, which have all attained a certain measure of technological and economic sophistication.

Premodern societies are generally characterized by a population that is diffused throughout numerous, small, and isolated pockets in rural or quasi-rural settings. There is little technological sophistication and little division of labor. Social relationships are personal, intimate, and essential, with the relations and institutions of kinship at the core of individual and social experience. Political hegemony is maintained by elites whose authority is based on traditional sanctions. The culture of the gemeinschaft is typically homogeneous; consequently social solidarity is based on similarity of role and of world view. All spheres of human life are bound by deeply rooted traditional modes of thought and behavior that are, almost without exception, religious or sacred in character. In contrast, modern societies are characterized by a population concentrated in urban areas. There is a highly intensified division of labor as well as a high degree of institutional specialization and segmentation. The economic sphere—the production apparatus in particular—is based on a highly sophisticated technology. Social relationships are largely impersonal and arbitrary; the primary mode of social organization in all spheres is bureaucratic. Political power is, at least ideologically, based in the populace. The gesellschaft is further characterized by sociocultural pluralism—a curious admixture of social and cultural worlds in various degrees of contact with one another. The world view of modern man is typically rational and secular, not bound by traditional sanctions but critical and open to innovation and experimentation. Solidarity in modern society is based on the interdependence fostered by role and institutional differentiation. Research based on the classical model gives special attention to the systematic description and elaboration of these ideal-typical constructs.

One of the criticisms leveled at the classical paradigm is that even if premodern societies are typologically different from modern societies, there is an entire range of variations in the manner and rate at which societies undergo transition. Historical variations are axiomatic. No two societies go through transition exactly alike, and this paradigm is insensitive to these substantive historical differences. Consonant with this criticism is the argument that this paradigm is Western-centric in the sense that it presumes that the Western pattern of modernization is the model or ultimate form of modernization toward which all societies aim and will converge. Critics maintain this is an assumption that cannot be justified simply on the basis of the West being first to undergo the process. Another criticism has been that the model presents the premodern–modern dichotomy in too exclusivistic terms, thereby not accounting for the carry-over of traditional forces or symbols even into the most modern social worlds.[3]

Significant problems certainly inhere within both models. Nonetheless, for the purposes of this undertaking, my approach is decidedly classical in its general theoretical contours. In defense of the classical paradigm, it is possible to avoid the aforementioned criticisms, for they are merely indicative of past tendencies and not foibles inherent in the model (Zijderveld, 1970:56). The primary reason for choosing the classical paradigm over the development paradigm is not any specific intellectual loyalty but suitability. Though the models are not mutually exclusive, the classical model provides the capacity for expeditious isolation and analysis of the core issues of the phenomenon under scrutiny. The development paradigm, on the other hand, invites cumbersome and ultimately superfluous detail in the analysis.

Therefore, *modernization* is to be understood here as a process of institutional change proceeding from and related to a technologically engendered economic growth. From this it follows that *modernity* is the evitable period in the history of a particular society that is characterized by the institutional and cultural concomitants of a technologically induced economic growth.[4] Though patently classical in its formulation, this definition does acknowledge that societies exist on a continuum of modernization. Societies can only be more or less modern on a continuum between ideal types. Following one scholar's usage, my distinctions are actually mainly between relatively nonmodern and relatively modern societies (Levy, 1966:9–11).

For the sake of theoretical clarity, my approach also must be contrasted with a third model, the Marxist one, which explains the peculiarity of modern institutions almost entirely in terms of the peculiar form of industrial capitalism. Where property relations are considered the determining variable in the Marxian model, my chosen approach assumes the ascendancy of the rationalized economy as the primary determining carrier of modernization, of which industrial capitalism is just one form. The elaboration of the chief institutional concomitants of a technologically induced economic growth, I leave until later.

Evangelicalism

Perhaps the most fundamental question about Evangelicalism is simply What is it? It may best be understood as a religiocultural phenomenon unique to North America, though clearly related in intimate ways to other forms of theologically conservative Protestantism in other times and places. The world view of Evangelicalism is deeply rooted in the theological tradition of the Reformation, in northern European Puritanism, and later in American Puritanism and the First and Second Great Awakenings in North America (Ballard, 1976; Marsden, 1980; McLoughlin, 1959). Indeed, Evangelicalism has striven to remain entirely faithful doctrinally to this general conservative tradition. At the doctrinal core, contemporary Evangelicals can be identified by their adherence to (1) the belief that the Bible is the inerrant Word of God, (2) the belief in the divinity of Christ, and (3) the belief in the efficacy of Christ's life, death, and physical resurrection for the salvation of the human soul. Behaviorally, Evangelicals are typically characterized by an individuated and experiential orientation toward spiritual salvation and religiosity in general and by the conviction of the necessity of actively attempting to proselytize all nonbelievers to the tenets of the Evangelical belief system.

To analyze Evangelicalism in the most general social-scientific sense, one might begin with Weber's (1958:95–154) typology of ascetic Protestantism: (1) Calvinism, with its special doctrinal emphasis on predestination and election; (2) Pietism, an essentially German phenomenon, with its emphasis on the spiritual perfection of the church on earth; (3) Anglo-American Methodism, with its emphasis on methodical but experiential personal conversion; and (4) the Baptist sects, with their doctrinal emphasis on personal salvation, the believer's church, and doctrinal repudiation of the notion of predestination. Elements of all four types are clearly found in the equally diverse contemporary Evangelicalism. There are four major religious and theological traditions in contemporary American Evangelicalism: (1) the Baptist tradition, (2) the Holiness-Pentecostal tradition, (3) the Anabaptist tradition, and (4) the Reformational-Confessional tradition.[5]

The Baptist tradition is distinguished by its highly individuated conception of human salvation (the notion of collective salvation—the salvation of the church—is foreign to this tradition). It maintains a belief in the importance of personal volition in the salvation process. Thus faith in general, salvation in particular, are highly subjectivized. Revivalism is most strongly evidenced in this religious heritage. Church structure in this tradition has tended toward the congregational type, which is to say toward a democratic (lay) form of church governance.

The Holiness-Pentecostal tradition maintains a very similar body of theological tenets and orientation toward ecclesiological structure. It is distinguished from the Baptist tradition, however, by its stronger emphasis on themes of pietism. The role of the Holy Spirit in the process of individual sanctification—the process of becoming spiritually purified and holy—is more salient here than in any other tradition. Perfectionist doctrines, moral and spiritual, distinguish the Holiness side of this tradition. The "second blessing" or the "baptism of the Holy Spirit" with the attendant "gifts of the Spirit" (glossolalia and xenoglosy in particular) are emphasized on the Pentecostal side.

The Anabaptist tradition, diverse within itself, nonetheless embodies general, unifying religious themes that distinguish it from the two aforementioned traditions.[6] Though maintaining an individuated conception of human salvation, the Anabaptist view is less subjectivistic in flavor. Faith is expressed in more objective and rational, as opposed to experiential, terms. Though the ecclesiastical structure found within this tradition is decidedly congregational as in the Baptist and Holiness-Pentecostal traditions, the Anabaptists emphasize the integration, interdependence, and solidarity of the church community over the rights and privileges of individual believers, a tendency found more in this than in any other tradition. The tradition has maintained a strong orientation toward social activism. Its most distinctive feature is its view of the relation of the church to the state. Where the other traditions tend to be supportive of the government structure and the activities of the broader society, the Anabaptist tradition maintains more of a neutral, if not antagonistic, posture toward the state and a particular opposition to war and violence of any sort.

The Reformational-Confessional tradition, like the Anabaptist tradition, though perhaps in some instances more so, tends to view faith and the salvation process in rational terms. On the Reformed side of the tradition the belief in divine predestination and election are still maintained, whereas these doctrines have little if any consequence on the Confessional side of this tradition. Asceticism and spiritual mastery are both stressed in the Reformational-Confessional tradition more than in any other Evangelical tradition. Church structure varies from the other traditions as well; ecclesiastical governance is more presbyterian or oligarchic.

Of the four traditions, the Baptist is presently the dominant one. The cultural style and theological flavor of this tradition is thus the most influential in defining the character of contemporary American Evangelicalism. Some of the differences between religious traditions are attributable to historical lineage. The Baptist tradition and the Holiness-Pentecostal tradition descend, by and large, from English pietism, dispensationalism, and millenarianism. The Reformational-Confessional and Anabaptist traditions descend from northern European, specifically Germanic Protestant, theological and religious movements. What they all share, true to the spirit of the Reformation, is a restorationist approach to religion. All four traditions have searched and continue to search for a purer, simpler, and more authentic form of religious experience, religious truth, and ecclesiastical authority, in other words, to recover the spirit and truth of the apostolic age of Christianity. At the heart of this effort is the Reformation principle of *sola scriptura*: the Word of God as the absolute authority in matters of religious, spiritual, and moral truth. Contemporary Evangelicalism, even in its diversity, remains committed to the quest to know and live Christianity in its authentic and divinely intended manner.

Evangelicalism encompasses sociological diversity as well. There have been efforts to construct social typologies of Evangelicals according to their social demeanor vis-à-vis the secular world and liberal Christianity or according to degree of dogmatism. The most important is Quebedeaux's (1974): separatist Fundamentalists, open Fundamentalists, establishment Evangelicals, the New Evangelicals, and the Young Evangelicals. This typology hinges on Quebedeaux's notion of etiquette (i.e., whether or not a type has "bad manners") and the extent to which a type is socially and politically "progressive." A more standard typology is a less refined distinction between Fundamentalists and Evangelicals (Barr, 1977). This typological distinction is more tenable inasmuch as it refers to a concrete historical phenomenon, yet even this distinction is not hard and fast. Although these efforts are prompted by genuine diversity, as typologies they fall short because the distinguishing parameters tend to be somewhat arbitrary and hazily drawn, with few if any concrete referents. Many of the distinctions are more adequately accounted for by social class and regional factors.

Sociology of Knowledge

An exploration of the relationship between Evangelicalism and modernity requires certain theoretical tools. For this undertaking, I have adopted the theoretical perspective of the *sociology of knowledge*. In its most basic formulation the sociology of knowledge is concerned with the relationship between human thought and social structure, in other words, with the social situation in which knowledge is found. The presumption is that the social structure largely determines the form and style of human thought—conversely, that the form and style of human thought largely reflect the social situation in which they are located. From the time of Karl Marx, however, the intellectual focus of the sociology of knowledge has generally been the social history of formal ideas and, more specifically, the social location and function of a variety of legitimating ideologies.

In the 1960s and 1970s, however, a major redefinition of the task of the sociology of knowledge has been advocated (P. Berger and Luckmann, 1966b; Holzner, 1968). The substance of this redefinition is, in a word, to shift the focus away from intellectual history and ideology to everything passing as knowledge in society—to the commonsense knowledge of everyday life without which social life could not be possible. It is this definition that I apply to this study of the relationship between Evangelicalism and modernity. My interest is in how they interact at the level of the world view of ordinary human beings—of the man on the street. Schutz (1976) offers a description of this ideal type:

> The man on the street has a working knowledge of many fields which are not necessarily coherent with one another. His is a knowledge of recipes indicating how to bring forth in typical situations typical results by typical means. The recipes indicate procedures which can be trusted even though they are not clearly understood. By following the prescription as if it were a ritual, the desired result can be attained without questioning why the single procedural steps have to be taken and taken exactly in the sequence pre-scribed. This knowledge in all its vagueness is still sufficiently precise for the practical purpose at hand. In all matters not connected with such practical purposes of immediate concern the man on the street accepts his sentiments and passions as guides. (p. 122)

For my purposes, an addition must be made to this ideal type. My con-cern is not with the world view of *any* man on the street but with that of the religious man on the street—the ordinary person who expressly derives ultimate meaning for his existence from sacred-supernatural symbols. His is a recipe knowledge of the workings of the cosmos—of the nature and man-ners of the gods; of the social, cultural, political, and economic realities in relation to the gods; and of his own place in this grand cosmologic scheme. Following Schutz (1976), this ideal type stands in contrast to two others: the *expert* (in this case, the theologian) and the *well-informed citizen* (the theologically trained layman). These are people with clear and distinct knowledge of the religious cosmology of which they are partisans. Their theological opinions and judgments are based on precise or reasonably pre-cise knowledge of the history and cartography of theological literature, issues, and policy. These two types are a relatively small percentage of the whole religious population; the examination of their world view would be, in the tradition of the earlier formulation of the sociology of knowledge, a sociology of modern theology. By concentrating my attention on the world view of ordinary people who are religious, I can describe the experience of a sig-nificantly larger population as they contend more or less unreflectively with the cognitive constraints of modernity.

2

Religion and Modernity:
A Sociology-of-Knowledge Approach

What are the consequences of modernity for religion? What are the circumstances brought about by the processes of modernization that prompt changes in the ways religion is manifested? What changes, if any, does religion undergo? The answers to these questions should contribute to an understanding of contemporary Evangelicalism. With few exceptions, most social-scientific research dealing with these questions has focused on the secularization of the social structure, that is, on the decrease of religious authority and influence in the political, economic, and educational spheres of collective life. Though this vast body of literature contributes greatly to our understanding of these questions, one might suppose from a look at contemporary affairs that there are other dynamics between modernity and religion than simply the institutional demise of the latter. Indeed there is evidence that suggests that a sort of bargaining takes place between the two, which can result in such possibilities as mutual accommodation, mutual permutation, or even symbiotic growth, taking place not only at the institutional but at the symbolic level—the level of world views. The theoretical interactions could include a multitude of empirical possibilities depending on the social, economic, and political conditions of modernization in a society and also on the historical, institutional, ethical, and intellectual characteristics of a particular religious tradition. Even so, there appear to be typical patterns of exchange or general tendencies, of which secularization of social structure and culture is just one.

Functional Rationality, Cultural Pluralism, and Structural Pluralism

Clearly there are innumerable elements of modernity that have affected religion. Three in particular have had considerable bearing on the sustained

11

existence and functionality of religion and religious world views: *functional rationality, cultural pluralism,* and *structural pluralism,* which is the division between the public and private spheres. The nature of these aspects of modernity and the constraints each imposes on religion have been examined at length by many others, making a cursory review sufficient here.

In the classical paradigm of modernization theory, it is generally held that at the core of economic and political modernization is the process of rationalization, by which is meant not "theoretical rationalization" as pertains to scientific and philosophic inquiry, but "functional rationalization," the infusion of rational controls through all spheres of human experience (Baum, 1970; Bell, 1976:10, 92; P. Berger et al., 1974:30 ff., 47 f., 202; Ellul, 1964; Marcuse, 1964). With functional rationality structurally institutionalized (in the form of technological production and the bureaucratic mode of social organization) and symbolically institutionalized (in the form of rational and utilitarian values) as perhaps the principal feature of modernity, how is religion affected at the level of subjective consciousness? What is the effect on the belief system of the ordinary religious person?

The assumption common in the literature is that the rationalization process is intrinsically inimical to religion at the level of subjective consciousness.[1] Whether intrinsically negative or not, empirically the assumption is usually borne out. Inasmuch as myth, magic, tradition, and authority are core elements of religion, the rationalization process, predicated as it is on a naturalistic metaphysic, is essentially undermining to the credibility of a religious orientation and thus contributes to what has been called the "disenchantment of the world."[2] Much empirical research has shown that the rationalization process does tend to corrode the believability of the religious meaning system. Thus it is increasingly difficult for people to maintain an open attachment to a perspective on reality the antithesis of which is institutionalized in most sectors of social life and taken for granted as the norm.[3] Religious belief and commitment are, as a result, much more tenuous for the man on the street.

A second key social-structural ornament of modernity with central relevance to the status of religion is cultural pluralism, the division of a society into subsocieties with more or less distinct cultural traditions (P. Berger, 1979:59; Fenn, 1970:131 f.; P. Hammond, 1974:118; Yinger, 1967:17). Of course the term does not suggest that each subculture is of equal status and power nor that the divisions are equally sharp, which clearly would not be true. What the term does imply is a form of social differentiation according to cultural systems that is a necessary concomitant of the modernization process.[4]

Institutionally, cultural pluralism is brought about by modern urbanization. The relatively modern city encompasses a broad spectrum of more or less distinct cultural traditions in close proximity to one another. This cultural diversity is also reflected in the modern media of mass communications: radio, television, motion pictures, mass publications, and so on. Hence one need not be in the city to experience it. The subjective dimension of this objective process is that modern people are constantly exposed to variant world views. Cultural pluralism at this level implies the collision between discrepant if not antagonistic perspectives on reality.[5]

Given that most religious world views are essentially monopolistic, cultural pluralism is likely to have a negative effect on them, and the evidence bears this out. The plurality radically undercuts the social support necessary for maintaining subjective adherence to a body of beliefs. Human beings require constant and present social confirmation to sustain their beliefs about reality, and where the social composition of a society is diversified, that social support necessarily dwindles.[6] The net effect is the rendering of a commitment to a certain world view precarious if not altogether implausible. The most fundamental and enduring experience a person is likely to encounter, then, is *cognitive dissonance*, an experience of confusion and anxiety about the certainty of his own understanding of reality. At the least, this leads to the questioning of the veracity of his beliefs and the consideration of the possibility of the truth of the beliefs of another ("There are gods other than my own. Is it possible that . . ."). Given a major collision of his view of reality with an alien conception in the absence of social conditions that confirm his own beliefs, it is highly probable that his beliefs will be compromised. He will feel constrained to modify aspects of his world view to account for this plurality in a conciliatory way.

The third major institutional concomitant of modernization with bearing on religion is structural pluralism, the historically unique dichotomization of life into public and private spheres (P. Berger, 1978b:130–141; P. Berger et al., 1974; P. Berger and Neuhaus, 1976; Cuddihy, 1974; Eisenstadt, 1966:3; Gehlen, 1957; Glennon, 1979; Habermas, 1974; Luckmann, 1967; Sennett, 1978). Constituting the setting of the public sphere are such massive institutions as the modern state, labor collectives, the professions, the educational as well as the scientific and technological bureaucracies, the health care bureaucracies and the military bureaucracies. Functional rationality defines the normative mode of thought, conduct, and social relationship in the public sphere. Thus these structures are often experienced as impersonal, abstract, and alienating. The area of human experience left over from the public sphere, including family life, primary social relationships, sexuality, personal identity, and meaning, constitute the setting of the private sphere. The private sphere is, therefore, typified by varying degrees of expressivity, particularity, and other subjective modes.

The principal constraint structural pluralism imposes on religion is *privatization*. Institutionally, privatization means that the influence of religious symbols and authority are routed out of one area of the public sphere after another. Religion is pressured into becoming depoliticized.[7] Its "proper" role is defined exclusively in terms of the satisfaction of personal or subjective needs. As an institution it is formally expected to provide subjectively meaningful interpretations of experience at the major events of the life cycle, a foundation for personal identity, and moral coordinates along which to order daily life. Thus religion has a legitimate role in modern life, but a role sharply circumscribed in relation to its former status in relatively non-modern situations.

At the subjective level of people's world views, the privatization of religion is internalized. Among other things this means that religious symbols and meanings tend to be relevant only within certain contexts of the modern person's everyday life, the moments spent in the private sphere. The highly rational character of the public sphere and the inutility and implausibility of religious definitions of reality in that context make it less likely that a person's religious beliefs will be relevant to him in such settings. Religion will seem much more viable in ordering his personal affairs.

All these institutional concomitants of modernization, then, have corrosive consequences for the establishment and maintenance of a religious world view. Put in different terms, all contribute in central ways to what could be called the *deinstitutionalization of religious reality* in the world views of modern people. If institutions pattern human thought, behavior, and social relations in a habitual and socially predictable manner, as well as provide human experience with an intelligibility and sense of continuity, then deinstitutionalization is the process whereby the patterns of human behavior and social relations become unstable and the commonsense coherence of traditionally valid reality definitions become unreliable and undependable. In human terms deinstitutionalization means that people are faced with an increasing number of choices concerning the manner in which to carry on the events of daily life. Modernity is characterized by an unprecedented degree of deinstitutionalization affecting all of the dimensions of private-sphere activity. Religious definitions of reality are particularly vulnerable to this process. The picture of the world presented in religious doctrine and symbols is not necessarily denied as a result of these structural tendencies, but is *disaffirmed* and therefore becomes less plausible in the minds of those confronting these forces. The truth or falseness of religion becomes a matter of individual choice.

Deinstitutionalization, then, is closely related to secularization. The deinstitutionalization of religious reality immediately precedes, indeed is a prerequisite of, the secularization of religious world views. Thus, the former is more widespread in modern societies than the latter. Although only a small percentage of modern people have abandoned a commitment to religious truth, most people in modern societies have at least become deeply perplexed by the ambiguities posed by these structural features of modernity.

Religious Repercussions: Cognitive Bargaining

In the face of the pressing dilemma posed by these institutional and symbolic components of modernity, what are the possible reactions of the average religious person with regard to his world view? Although detailed answers must be sought in the substantive details of specific cases, generally speaking there are two basic options: resistance and accommodation. There is also a third option, of course: withdrawal—avoiding the confrontation with modernity entirely by refusing to participate in the modern social system and in modern culture in every way possible. A good example of this is the Amish community's attempt at almost total isolation. This option is not possible, however, nor even desirable, for most religious groups. The adherents of most religions in the West must actively participate in the modern setting, leaving them the options of resistance or accommodation. This is to say that the adherents of a religious world view may either attempt to resist the compromising realities of modernity or attempt to make the best of the situation by giving in to modernity's cognitive pressures. Of course there is between these two ideals a continuum of possibility on which most empirical cases lie. In any case, however, a fundamental premise here is that there is a constant causal reciprocity between consciousness and social structure and therefore that interaction between religious world views and the structures and processes of modernity will be a sociological necessity. At the level of consciousness, the dynamics of this interaction may be labeled *cognitive bargaining*.

It is theoretically possible, of course, that religious world views could affect the direction and structure of modernity. Yet in this dialectical interchange, it is safe to say that the religious world view is the weaker partner. In other words, it is likely that the cognitive bargaining between the structures and processes of modernity and a religious belief system taking place in the arena of people's world views would result in *cognitive contamination* of the religious world view.[8] This would be due to the massive plausibility structures available for the modern rational and secular world view and the comparatively small and fragile plausibility structures available for any form of religious world view. Empirically, there would still be a variety of reactions depending on such factors as the ethical content of the religious world view and the social base of the religious group espousing it. In spite of specific resistances, nonetheless, the onus of pressure would be on the adherents of the religious world view to accommodate to the cognitive constraints of modernity by modifying the content and style of their beliefs. Even within religious traditions that are unusually intransigent—that is, resistant to these pressures (the orthodox and conservative traditions)—a measure of accommodation is predictable. Unless there is total avoidance of these processes, reciprocal interchange between consciousness and social structure will occur, and the cognitive constraints of modernization are much too great for even an orthodoxy to avoid some form of adaptation.

Accommodation to the cognitive constraints of functional rationality would probably express itself in a variety of ways, some of which I have already suggested. For one thing, there would be specific pressures on adherents to demythologize the supernatural elements of their world view. The most extreme accommodation would be total reinterpretation of the religious cosmology into the grammar of naturalism, as for example, in the translation of Christianity into ethics, psychology, and currently, politics by some liberal and "radical" theologians. A less radical accommodation would be the reduction in frequency of references to the supernatural substance of the belief system, as adherents played down the more extravagant-seeming supernaturalistic conceptions. This sort of accommodation might also manifest itself as an increased tendency toward an inner-worldly, utilitarian orientation. Finally, adherents might increase their attempts to provide rational explanations for their beliefs. A rise in apologetic activity can be understood as a tacit recognition of a growing implausibility of religious authority. All of these adjustments would be prompted by the need to reduce the distance between the "real" and the "ideal" in order to make personal belief more credible.[9]

Accommodation to the cognitive pressures of sociocultural pluralism would be another matter. A variety of competing religious world views all claiming a monopoly on ultimate truth would inevitably create friction. The likely result would be a cognitive bargaining ending in compromises of varying degree on all fronts. The specific pressure cultural pluralism brings to bear on the adherents of a particular religious cosmology is the pressure to recognize and acknowledge the monopolistic claims of another. A structural solution is privatization. Treating religious belief as merely a matter of personal preference makes it unlikely that contradictory beliefs will have the occasion to surface in the course of social exchange. Yet privatization generally only solves the problem of pluralism in its political dimensions, not at the cognitive level. The modern person is still left with the nagging question Which beliefs are the correct ones?

One option is to claim that the existence of diverse religious cosmologies relativizes each one's claim to singularity and absoluteness; the specific religious content of all the traditions are therefore necessarily false. Another possibility is to claim that all religious traditions are true inasmuch as they all share common core elements. Each specific religious heritage is, then, just one of many possibilities through which these common truths find expression. Liberal tendencies in theology are largely predicated on this belief. Both of these options constitute a forthright accommodation to the cognitive constraints of sociocultural pluralism.

A final option is cognitive intransigence—ignoring the plurality by affirming the veracity of one tradition and the illegitimacy of the others. Evangelicalism pursues this option. But even in this situation where the resistance is greatest, some yielding is likely. Over time, the purported defenders of the faith would be inclined to become more tolerant of other religious traditions even while maintaining their firm commitment to their own beliefs as the one and only truth. This increased tolerance might be expressed as a willingness to associate with adherents of another tradition without insisting on proselytizing—a softening of the dogmatic insistence on conversion (i.e., "God is a just God. Who am I to pass judgment? Let Him be the Judge").

Structural pluralism and the corresponding privatization of religion would result in specific pressure on adherents to play down the public import of their world view. It would therefore be reasonable to expect them to de-emphasize to some degree the more charismatic and prophetic elements of their world view as they pertain to public issues. There would also be corresponding pressure to inflate the relevance of religious norms and values to the affairs of the private sphere.

The Protest against Modernity

Accommodation is only one result of the bargaining that is likely to occur between religion and modernity. While a measure of accommodation is predictable, social scientists have suggested that modernity creates circumstances that evoke resistance to itself (Bellah, 1976; P. Berger et al., 1974; Zijderveld, 1972). When the world-disaffirming qualities inhering in modernity (the anomie resulting from massive deinstitutionalization in the private sphere and the alienation from the abstract overinstitutionalized structures of the public sphere) reach a certain level, modern people will resist or protest against these discontents. Resistance to modernity may and often does take political and cultural form, but it may also take religious form.[10] Forceful resurgences of personal piety and personal religious commitment may occur under such conditions. The rise of the new religious movements exemplifies this. Yet such recharismatization would inevitably be almost exclusively a private-sphere phenomenon—an effort to buttress a strained and enfeebled private world. Though resurgences of religiosity do occur in the private sphere, the ever-present forces of modernity undermine their active and sustained presence. Thus it is conceivable that cycles of religiosity and secularism can occur under the conditions of modernity.[11]

A question arises, however, in response to a plethora of literature that speaks of the viable presence in some relatively modern societies of a "civil religion." This issue has particular bearing on the case of American Evangelicalism. The concept of *civil religion* expresses a body of quasi-religious doctrine that has the capacity to be both an integrative force in the presence of an intense sociocultural pluralism and a legitimating agency of the modern state. As such, it can be understood as primarily a religious ideology of the public sphere. Does the presence of civil religion contradict the idea that traditional religious symbols can only really thrive in the private sphere in highly modern societies?

The answer is not clear, but there are clues. One scholar (Parsons, 1963; cf. Fenn, 1970:30) points to the historical tendency of less general, particularistic values to be overcome by more universal values as societies modernize. In the American situation the specific orientations of particular (denominational) religious traditions give way to the more general value system of the Judeo-Christian tradition, which then becomes institutionalized within the social structure.[12] Particular religious symbols and values become attenuated and diffused into a more general, more nebulous body of doctrine that bears varying degrees of resemblance to the original traditions. The political exigencies of sociocultural pluralism demand nothing less.[13]

Where civil religion does emerge, however, it should be understood as something very different from the creed of a particular religious tradition regardless of any ideological affinities, as evidence on the nature of American civil religion overwhelmingly shows.[14] It is unlikely, however, that the religious man on the street makes this distinction. In fact, the adherents of a particular religious world view would probably identify public religious activism as an essential part of their belief system. Whereas in most cases the presence of civil religious symbols can be understood as the cultural residue of the society in an earlier period, more extreme civil religious activism can be understood as an expression of the protest against modernity, as a reaction to a secularized public sphere, and as an attempt to reconcile the disjunctive worlds of the public and private spheres. Thus, traditional religious symbols can surface in the public sphere but typically in attenuated form. Survival of this public-sphere religiosity depends almost entirely on the plausibility structures of the private sphere. Thus, the more modern a setting, the more sporadic and ephemeral any civil religious activism.

In answering the questions concerning the relationship between religion and modernity posed at the start of this chapter, I have argued that a type of bargaining takes place in which religion is forced to deal with the constraints the modernity imposes. Though the general direction of these relationships seems clear enough, there are, of course, limitless contingencies that would affect the status of a particular religious cosmology at a particular time. As a result, there is no single pattern of secularization or even accommodation constant for all religions in all situations, nor is there any single and uniform expression of religious resistance to modernity. The specific relation between modernity and religion would have to be determined empirically in each case. This study, of course, concerns the dynamics of this relationship in one case, a faction of American Protestantism.

Within American Protestantism the theologically liberal faction has received the greatest amount of scholarly attention. It has been recognized for fashioning new and uncharted theological directions in this relationship. Theologically conservative Protestantism in America is, on the other hand, usually dismissed as an anachronism, as a marginal remnant of an outdated form of religious consciousness and lifestyle. In many circles, it is assumed that conservative Protestantism will soon see its final dissolution. Whatever its fate, this form of religious world view has had a unique history and its own unique encounter with the processes of modernization.

Part Two

SOCIAL AND HISTORICAL BACKGROUND

3

History of a World View, 1890 to the Present

Traditional historiography on American Evangelicalism is dominated by several pervasive but unsubstantiated themes. One such theme is that Evangelicalism has always been a working-class and lower middle-class "agrarian protest movement centered in the South," incited and maintained by "ill-taught stump preachers or demagogues" (Sandeen, 1968:26). Another theme, which provides the basis for the first, is that Evangelicalism as a form of religious world view has little historical relation, and as such bears little resemblance, to eighteenth- and nineteenth-century American Protestantism. The historical background of contemporary American Evangelicalism, it is thus maintained, can be adequately understood by reference to its "beginnings" in the tumultuous decade of the 1920s and the events that followed.

Yet careful treatment of this phenomenon reveals the inadequacies of this understanding. The principal thesis in this chapter is that what is now known as contemporary American Evangelicalism (1) is a socioreligious phenomenon rooted historically in the mainstream (not the sectarian margin) of the nineteenth-century American Protestant experience and (2) was subsequently shaped by and in reaction to the symbolic and structural constraints of modernity—a process that began well before the sensationalism of the 1920s. A more suitable starting point than the 1920s is the period known by many scholars as perhaps the last enduring acme of American Protestantism. A more appropriate emphasis is on accounting for changes in the Evangelical world view by referring to simultaneous modernizing changes in American culture and society.

The Gilded Age of American Protestantism

Nineteenth-century Protestant orthodoxy, or Evangelicalism as it was then called, was not just one religious world view among many. In the direct line of succession from the colonial religious temper and the First and Second

23

Great Awakenings, its ethical and interpretive system, formally institutionalized within the denominational structure, was unquestionably predominant, not only in the religious life of America, but in the broader culture.[1] The nineteenth-century Evangelical held to be normative the core religious beliefs of reformational orthodoxy: an individuated conception of personal salvation mediated by Jesus Christ, the role of the Bible as the sole authority on religious and spiritual matters, the need for obedience to the sovereign will of God in his vocation and in his personal and family life. In addition he maintained the conviction of the superiority of the Christian (which always meant "Protestant") faith.

Central to the religious life of the nineteenth-century Evangelical was the revival. An important mode of religious renewal in Protestantism during the eighteenth century, revivalism increased in vitality through most of the nineteenth century until it became one of the central cultural ornaments of the period. Beginning with the Second Great Awakening in 1800 to 1802 and its follow-up after the War of 1812, large-scale revivals can be traced through the late 1820s, the era of Charles G. Finney (1825–1835), the revivals between 1837 and 1857, the layman's revival of 1858, and the revivals of Dwight L. Moody (1870–1892) (Handy, 1971:29; Hudson, 1961:177–182; Marty, 1970:121; McLoughlin, 1959, 1968). Revivalism, which found expression in most of the denominations,[2] largely accounted for the unity of style and substance of Protestant life during this period.

A distinct though not unrelated element of the nineteenth-century Evangelical world view was the Protestant ethical orientation expressed in ascetic self-discipline (chastity, temperance, and the like), frugality, industry, pragmatism, and so on. This ethical orientation had particular import in the spheres of work and commerce, but in every way it spawned an optimism about the future of mankind.

Theological and ethical elements woven together formed the basic fabric of the world view dominant in this period of American history, a world view that found its primary social support in the small towns of mercantile America (Bell, 1976:56; Marty, 1970:162, 169). But these two elements were not equally represented; differences of emphasis were sometimes major depending on such variables as region and class. Thus, though the theological and ethical elements together constituted the fabric of the nineteenth century American world view, the pattern was not entirely uniform.

Another important aspect of this tapestry was the notion held by the majority that America was a nation set apart for a divine purpose. America was seen as the "new" Israel; Americans, having a covenant with God, were the chosen people entrusted with the responsibility of establishing a "righteous empire" or a Christian commonwealth within this new land (Handy, 1971; Hudson, 1961:109 ff.; Marty, 1970). To be sure, these convictions derived to a considerable extent from the historical precedent of

Europe, where the notion of the Christian civilization had been firmly rooted since the fourth century. The nineteenth-century American Evangelical could scarcely view society as striving to be anything else. A further reason, however, could be that the larger part of the immigrating population was made up of dissenting Protestant groups. America was a place where such groups could escape social, economic, and often physical persecutions. The biblical metaphor of being led from captivity to a land of possibility and fortune was therefore bound to be a recurrent feature of American folklore, particularly in the nineteenth century.

Although nineteenth-century American society was formally committed to the principle of separation of church and state and to voluntarism as the means of sustaining religion, the notion of the quest for a Christian America was, nonetheless, firmly institutionalized. Local, state, and federal governments, dominated in the main by people who shared this conviction, were thus structured to encourage its ascendancy within the culture. With industry and commerce also dominated by those of this mold, the result was the establishment of a uniquely Protestant style of life and work (and therefore, world view) in American society as a whole, even non-Protestant portions of it. Christianization also occurred in the educational system, especially at the lower levels. It effectively functioned to socialize large elements of the population into the values and expectations of mainstream Evangelical America. Indeed, even conversion at a revival often served as a rite of passage by which the recent immigrant would enter the American mainstream.

Yet the vision of the Christian empire went beyond the political boundaries of the United States. The vision was of the Christianization of the entire world. Even as late as 1890, Lewis Stearns declared:

> Today Christianity is the power which is moulding the destinies of the world. The Christian nations are in the ascendant. Just in proportion to the purity of Christianity as it exists in the various nations of Christendom is the influence they are exerting upon the world's destiny. The future of the world seems to be in the hands of the three great Protestant powers—England, Germany, and the United States. The old promise is being fulfilled; the followers of the true God are inheriting the world. (Handy, 1971:121)

Where the interpretive view of the nineteenth-century American Evangelical played an important role in the legitimation of American imperialistic initiatives, the Christian missionary effort played a central role in actuating those initiatives. As several social and historical commentators have maintained, the "thought of Puritan theocracy" established in the United States and worldwide "is the great influential fact in the history of the American mind" (Bell, 1976:56).

On all of these points there was widespread consensus. A number of more specific beliefs and ideas were less generally held. Three general religious themes are discernible in nineteenth-century Evangelicalism. One was constituted by the Reformed, or Calvinist, heritage. Doctrinal emphasis at this time followed strictly orthodox themes. At the fore was the belief in the absolute sovereignty of God in individual and historical affairs. Human efforts in history occurred only through divine Providence, and human ability played little if any role in personal salvation. Heaven was a gift of God to those he foreordained to receive grace. This heritage also tended toward a postmillennial view of history. Corresponding to the emphasis on right doctrine was the practical emphasis on educational training and development of the intellect. The Confession of Faith and the Catechism of the Westminster Assembly were taught to Presbyterian and Reformed youth. Memorization of the Shorter Catechism at an early age was common practice. A third emphasis was ecclesiological. Related to the distinct Reformed theological tradition was the denominational pursuit of a strong and vast church structure, which had important consequences for what was to follow later in the century. It was out of this general tradition that nineteenth-century American revivalism developed (Marsden, 1980:7).

A second major theme was *millennialism*. As one historian (Sandeen, 1970b) points out, America in the early nineteenth century was "drunk on the millenium" (cf. Dayton, 1980). As with most religious beliefs, Christian eschatology in the early part of the nineteenth century was not formalized in a theological system, nor was it clearly defined in terms of any specific Protestant tradition. There were a variety of beliefs concerning the end of times. The postmillennial view optimistically maintained that the stage was being set in the present era for a thousand-year reign of peace and justice (spoken of in the Book of Revelations) *after* which Christ would return. Premillennialism, on the other hand, anticipated the dramatic bodily return of Christ on earth only when the degenerating effects of man's sinful rebellion against God reached the depths. The Second Advent would signal the end of sin and death and the vanquishing of Satan as well as the inauguration of a peaceful kingdom lasting a thousand years. Divine judgment would then follow. Both postmillennial and premillennial views of history existed side by side in most denominations in mid-nineteenth-century America (though postmillennialism was clearly predominant before the Civil War). Premillennialism, however, was gaining increasing acceptance.[3] Though premillennial views were widely discredited as a result of the sectarian Millerites, who donned ascension robes in anticipation of the Second Advent in 1844, those holding such views did organize loosely into a movement toward the end of the century, publishing periodicals and holding annual conferences.

In time, the premillenarian movement became associated with dispensationalism, a theological system popularized in the nineteenth century by a Church of Ireland expatriate, John Nelson Darby. Dispensationalism stressed not only a premillennial eschatology but a unique historiography in which human history was classified into specific dispensations, or historical eras, each dominated by a prevailing principle. Each dispensation ends in conflict, divine judgment on those who rule, and the introduction of a wholly new era (Marsden, 1980:64). Dispensationalism, though not originating in this way, came to tend toward an Arminian (free will) as opposed to Calvinistic (deterministic) approach to salvation. The adoption of premillennialism by the dispensationalists further solidified millenarianism as a recognizable movement. As the movement grew in size, it also gained in respectability. By the end of the nineteenth century, dispensational millenarianism had become perhaps the dominant religious theme in conservative Protestantism (Dayton, 1980; Marty, 1970:216 f.; Sandeen, 1970b:227).

A third theme in the religious tapestry of nineteenth-century America was *holiness teachings*. Emerging at this time essentially from the Wesleyan tradition, the holiness teachings emphasized sanctification by the Holy Ghost. Many people considered spiritual perfection attainable; the sinful nature, eradicable. The dominant influence, however, was provided by the Keswick movement, whose leaders taught that perfection could only be approximated through constant fillings of the Holy Spirit.

Each of these themes, though analytically distinct, influenced each other in significant ways. Doctrinal factions and theological disputes (especially those on the nature of the millennium) were of importance not only to church leaders but to growing numbers of church people as well. In spite of diversity, the basic strength and unity of the doctrinal character and religious style of the nineteenth-century world view, so emphatically conservative Protestant, could be taken for granted as normative. But though Protestantism entered the period just before the turn of the century with this good measure of stability, it also clearly displayed signs of stress in its monopoly on the culture.

The Disestablishment of American Protestantism, 1890–1919

Toward the end of the nineteenth century, the perplexing realities of modernization imposed themselves with increasing intensity. The social and economic problems associated with industrialization and urbanization (e.g., crowded and inadequate housing, conditions of labor in the factory system, a changing family structure, increasing crime and suicide rates, and so on) could no longer be ignored, nor could the religious and cultural pluralism brought by the unprecedented influx of Irish and Italian (Roman Catholic) and Eastern European (Jewish) immigrants. Among the Protestant leadership there was at first a widespread recognition of these problems and the threat they posed to Protestant hegemony but an equally pervasive confidence and enthusiasm about their rectification. As Handy (1971) has written, "it was believed that good intentions and an abundance of zeal would with God's help be adequate to handle the difficult problems" (p. 143). Nonetheless, this confidence soon gave way to anxiety and to discontent with traditional understandings and solutions to these problems—a discontent that was to adumbrate a formal split in American Protestantism and the demonopolization of conservative Protestant faith in America.

Pressure was also coming from the university. From the time of Friedrich Schleiermacher in the late eighteenth century, intellectuals in Europe and to a lesser extent in the United States had been grappling with the issues posed by modern rationality and religious pluralism and thus with the modern world view. The historical resolution on the part of the theological community had been a general accommodation signaled by, among other things, the progressive abandonment of supernaturalism and the relativization and equalization of all religious belief systems. For the general clergy and the man on the street, these occurrences bore little if any consequence until close to the end of the nineteenth century, when rumors of this theological accommodation began, in Nietzsche's words, "to reach the ears of men."

The response to these pressures was gradual just as the building of pressure had been gradual; it first appeared in the ranks of the general clergy. While there still existed a unilateral effort among all Protestants backing missions and the reform of such vices as intemperance, prostitution, and profanity, increasing numbers of the clergy representing all denominations began to advocate in addition a "New Christianity" and a "new theology." These were purported to be based on the interpretive inadequacies of their predecessors. As Walter Rauschenbusch, a late nineteenth-century advocate of the New Christianity put it, "when I had begun to apply my previous religious ideas to the conditions I found, I discovered that they didn't fit" (Marty, 1970:185). Largely a composite of two closely related movements, the social gospel and cooperative Christianity, the New Christianity was an attempt to deal with the growing perplexities of modern life in what its advocates believed to be a creative and responsible fashion. Advocates of the social gospel repudiated an individuated conception of moral and social ills in favor of an interpretation of such phenomena as resulting from social, political, and economic realities over which the individual had little or no control.[4] Correspondingly, they saw the basis of reform as not so much the revival—where, so they believed, the "hearts of men would be purged from sin"—as the modification of the structural conditions precipitating these social maladies. Providing the basis of authority for such a perspective was the Bible infused with a nearly exclusive social meaning.

Though the first articulation of the social gospel could be traced to the 1870s in the works of such as Washington Gladden, Walter Rauschenbusch, Robert Ely, and later, Josiah Strong, it was not until the 1890s that the social gospel began to emerge as a movement with force and to gain respectability in the life of the denominations. This acceptance is evident in both the growth of popularity of social gospel literature and the spawning of new organizations such as the Brotherhood of the Kingdom, the Department of Church and Labor of the Presbyterian Church's Board of Home Missions, the Methodist Federation for Social Service, and the commission on the Church and Social Service, and the publication of such documents as the Social Creed of the Churches.

A second feature of the New Christianity was a movement in Protestantism known as "cooperative Christianity." A number of attempts had been made to form an independent organization to unify church bodies on a broad scale, for example, the Evangelical Churches of Christendom in 1900 and the National Federation of Churches and Christian Workers in 1901. But it was not until 1908, with the founding of the Federal Council of the Churches of Christ in America (the FCC) that these efforts achieved an enduring success. As a national interchurch agency, the FCC was to function as the effective means by which social and political reform could be organized on behalf of the churches. Among other things, the interfaith cooperation marked by the founding of the FCC also represented a move toward interfaith toleration and ecumenism (Cavert, 1968; Handy 1971:170 ff.).

Formal theologizing was an activity generally unsuited to the tastes of the nineteenth-century American Evangelical. Even among ecclesiastical leaders and intellectuals, academic theological inquiry was not pursued with nearly the vigor and depth it was in Europe, particularly Germany. Princeton Seminary was, of course, a notable exception. By the turn of the century, however, American interest in formal theology was on the rise on all fronts.[5] Out of this interest emerged a "new theology." As a movement in intellectual circles concomitant with many of the ideological and structural changes occurring within the church at large, the new theology greatly functioned to legitimate the latter. Yet in addition the new theology advocated a synthesis of the major scientific findings within Christian thought (Darwinism and social Darwinism most notably) as well as a social (often brazenly naturalistic) interpretation of the biblical writings.

The New Christianity and the new theology in the 1890s were not by any means popularly embraced by the majority of American Protestants. These changes took hold among church leaders and intellectuals primarily in the urban regions of the Northeast, where the processes of modernization were especially accelerated and the social and economic effects of modernity were most visible (Marty, 1970:154, 170, 172, 183). Thus, these changes only account for part of the activity within Protestantism during this period.

In the 1890s the majority of Protestants continued to hold to a traditional orthodoxy, and from the ecclesiastical leadership there emerged a

loosely organized movement dedicated to defending orthodoxy from the pernicious doctrines of the New Christianity. The movement derived its structure and direction principally from the premillennialists—men such as
Moody, A. J. Gordon, James Brookes, Arno Gaebelein, Charles G. Trum-
bull, Arthur T. Pierson, Rueben Torrey, and C. I. Scofield—and to a lesser
extent from the Princeton Calvinists—men such as Archibald Alexander
Hodge, Charles Hodge, and B. B. Warfield. Like the New Christianity and
the new theology, this movement was also centered in the metropolitan
sectors of the Northeast.

Although most of the members of this movement shared a concern for
the problems of industrialization and urbanization, they never really offered
an extensive social reformism. This proved to be something of a shift in
policy inasmuch as nineteenth-century Evangelicalism typically emphasized a balanced concern for the spiritual and social needs of men. This
shift, which has been labeled "the great reversal," was largely a result of the
decline in the influence of postmillennial traditions and the rise of the premillenarian influences in the denominations as a whole (Dayton, 1976;
Marsden, 1980:85 ff.; Moberg, 1972; Smith, 1976). In any event, one of
the only successful attempts by conservative Evangelicals to deal directly
with these problems at this time was the effort of the Salvation Army, an
imported offshoot from British Wesleyanism. In the main, however, conservative Evangelicals reacted (in keeping with premillennial eschatology)
with a sustained pessimism toward the period owing to their view that the
trials of the age were evidences of humankind's total depravity and of the
approaching Second Coming of Christ and the end of time. Thus, their
greatest preoccupation became the salvation of souls. The archetypal social
ministry became, at this time, the "rescue mission," in which the goal was
to "rescue" people or call them out from the sin and degradation of the
culture (Dayton, 1980:14). Though there was not nearly as much energy
and enthusiasm behind mass revivalism at the end of the nineteenth century,
it still showed signs of vitality (McLoughlin, 1959). Moody's revivals continued into the early 1890s followed soon and continuing through the first
two decades of the new century by the mass evangelism of the extravagant
ex-baseball player, Billy Sunday (McLoughlin, 1955). Missions also continued to be dominated by the conservatives. The important Student Volunteer Movement is most notable in this regard.

Advocates of the traditional orthodoxy typically suspected anyone outside
of their camp with flirting with apostasy, and this was especially so for the
proponents of the New Christianity. What troubled conservatives about the
social gospel in particular was not the endorsement of social concern but
the emphasis on social concern to the exclusion of the spiritual dimensions
of faith (Marsden, 1980:92). Thus, the slow-growing popularity of the New
Christianity was recognized by the conservatives and feared as a veritable

threat to the ascendancy of the apostolic faith. In this regard, conservatives considered the protection of the divine nature of the Bible at the center of their defense. They generally reasoned that, if they successfully defended the notion that the Bible was the inerrant and infallible Word of God, to be interpreted literally as such, then an adequate basis would exist for dismissing all erroneous teachings.

Yet, as Sandeen (1970b) pointed out, a fully integrated theology of biblical authority did not exist in Protestantism during the major part of the nineteenth century.

> What did exist was a great deal of popular reverence for the Bible, the eighteenth-century literature defending the authenticity of the scriptures and providing "evidences" of their supernatural origin . . . and an apologetic stance which had conditioned defenders of the faith to respond to any challenge to the Bible with the cry "heresy." (p. 106).

A systematic theology defending the infallibility of the Bible had to be created, and one was created in the latter part of the nineteenth century, primarily through the efforts of the Princeton Calvinists, Hodge and Warfield most notably. The Princeton doctrine of the Scriptures was intellectually complementary to the hermeneutic literalism of the dispensational millennialists and therefore served to imbue the latter with intellectual credence.

Conservatives established other lines of cognitive defense as well; one was higher education. Before the 1880s all higher education was controlled by Protestant denominations, their primary vocation being the training and certification of ministers, teachers, revivalists, and the like. Thus, institutions of higher education were bastions of Evangelical unity and strength. After this time, however, a trend toward the secularization of higher education began. Religion departments formed and were segregated from other departments; an increasing number of secular courses of study (the sciences, in particular) were introduced; and compulsory chapel was discontinued. In response, Bible institutes and colleges emerged with the expressed intention of training ministers, missionaries, and lay people in the defense and extension of the central doctrines of the Christian faith (Hudson, 1961:118; Marty, 1970:202; Sandeen, 1970b:183). Among such institutions could be listed the Moody Bible Institute in Chicago, the Northwestern Bible Training School in Minneapolis, the Bible Institute of Los Angeles, the Toronto Bible Training School, and the Philadelphia Bible Institute. Frequent conferences, such as the Niagara Bible Conferences, the American Bible and Prophetic Conference, the Northfield Conferences, the Old Point Comfort Bible Conference, and the Seaside Bible Conference, also became an institutionalized feature of conservative Protestant life. A final means of shoring up the cognitive defense was the scores of periodicals dedicated to propagating orthodox views. Among them were *Waymark in the Wilderness,*

Prophetic Times, *American Millenarian and Prophetic Review*, *Bible Champion*, and *Watchword and Truth*.

The efforts of conservatives to protect orthodoxy from the influence of the New Christianity slowly proved inadequate. By the second decade of the twentieth century, the greater part of Protestant ministers and theologians had abandoned the conservative position as indefensible. The accommodating forces in Protestantism had not been contained. Conservatives had difficulties in effectively organizing. They were beset by an old and dying leadership without competent replacements, and they were at the same time preoccupied by a variety of in-house doctrinal disputes. The future of the conservative Evangelical tradition in America was clearly uncertain. Notwithstanding these perplexities, conservatives launched in 1910 a major effort (though not the last) to regain a cognitive grasp over Protestantism with the publication of *The Fundamentals* (Hudson, 1961:148; Marsden, 1980: 118 ff.; Sandeen, 1970b:188–207).

Sponsored by two wealthy conservative Protestant businessmen, the twelve volumes (containing ninety articles) of *The Fundamentals* were designed to check the spread of the New Christianity. They systematically covered doctrinal issues relating to the inerrancy of the Scriptures (the doctrine of inspiration, archaeological confirmation of biblical stories, and the refutation of higher criticism), other Christian doctrines (the existence of God, the historicity of Christ, the nature of the Holy Spirit, the personal premillennial return of Christ, and the nature of the Christian life), commentary on the need for missions and evangelism, and finally, refutations of other religious systems (including Mormonism, Christian Science, spiritualism and Roman Catholicism). Though *The Fundamentals* was widely dispersed among church leaders, it was generally ignored by the academic and scholarly community. Its net accomplishment of its stated goals was dubious; at best, it provided a pause in the trend toward the decline of conservative power in the denominations.

Naturally, the chronicling of past events is made easier by reflection from a future point. What later seems to be a clear progression of events is at the time seen as a series of events and ideas that appear as expressions of unconscious and often unplanned actions with no sure design. In retrospect it is now clear that the period from just before the turn of the century through the end of World War I was a most decisive one for American Protestantism. By 1919, it was clear even to the man on the street that a bifurcation had emerged within American Protestantism. On the one hand, there were the purported defenders of Protestant orthodoxy, now ignobly labeled "Fundamentalists" after the publication. On the other hand, there were the "Modernists," the advocates of the New Christianity and the new theology who had initiated innovations in Protestant belief that were allegedly more attuned to the progressive spirit of the times. As a carry-over from the nineteenth century, the conservative forces had enjoyed wide popular respect and support and maintained their status as a cognitive majority, while the liberalizing forces slowly emerged from an enfeebled beginning to become a recognizable yet minority movement through the first decade of the twentieth century. By 1919, however, not only had the split widened but popular support for the two sides had begun to reverse. Conservative forces had plainly lost the cognitive grasp on the American population as a whole and on Protestantism in particular, and the progressive ideas of Protestant liberalism were making incremental gains.

In reviewing this chronology of events, one can now understand the New Christianity and the new theology as a decided capitulation to the cognitive constraints of modernity at two levels of sophistication, the popular and the intellectual. Perhaps the distinguishing characteristic of the former was a shift in emphasis from the spiritual to the social and practical. The spiritual needs of humankind were to be treated not necessarily as paramount but as one set among many. This indicated, among other things, a growing doubt concerning the plausibility and viability of a more spiritualistic interpretation of human experience as opposed to a more philosophically rational and naturalistic perspective. More than a tacit capitulation to the cognitive constraints of religious pluralism, the fledgling ecumenism of the New Christianity also marks a devaluation of the spiritual (the quest for doctrinal purity) in favor of a cooperatively based social reformism. As I have mentioned, the new theology provided an intellectual legitimation for the liberalizing changes in Protestantism. But in its own right, the new theology (higher criticism and the like) signaled an acquiescence to the cognitive constraints of modern scientific rationalism—the desire to make sense of the biblical literature in light of modern philosophical rationalism and the desire to make reasonable the Christian world view in the presence of hard, seemingly contradictory evidence. The New Christianity and the new theology must, then, be understood as a direct response to the cognitive constraints imposed by the modernization process, a response that was to make Christianity more compatible with the still-inchoate modern world view.

In examining the conservative movement in Protestantism, one must pose the uneasy question: Were they really defending the apostolic faith or reformational orthodoxy? All too often, the affirmative claims of the conservatives go unquestioned. On closer scrutiny the answer is not so apparent; in fact, the opposite is closer to the truth. Though most conservative Protestants may have started out in the last decades of the nineteenth century defending American Protestant orthodoxy, it is evident that, by 1919, they espoused something of a variant of it. How was this?

If the New Christianity can be understood as a conciliatory response to the cognitive pressure of modern institutional structures and processes, Fundamentalism must also be understood as a reaction to modernity. On the one hand, there was the reaction to the calamities associated with industrialization and urbanization. The postmillennialist vision of a "world growing better and better" became untenable to many in this context. The premillennialism view of a "world growing worse and worse" was much more plausible (Dayton, 1980). Indeed premillennialism as a cognitive response to modernity not only came to dominate late nineteenth-century conservative Protestantism but came to determine much of its future character. On the other hand there was the reaction to the modern world view as represented by theological Modernism. Conservative forces in the nineteenth century had no significant quarrel with the institutional changes occurring at that time. Neither did the earlier Baconian view of science or even the modern secular world view pose any serious threat to conservative Protestant hegemony in the culture at that point.[6] It was only when the presence of the modern world view became internal to Protestantism (in the form of Modernism) that the threat became imminent (Marsden, 1980:159). In response, conservative forces sought to defend those aspects of orthodoxy that they regarded as absolutely fundamental to its longevity: the infallibility of Scripture, the deity and yet the historicity of Christ and his mission, personal salvation as the paramount concern for every person, and therefore the need for the evangelization of the world, and finally, the bodily return of Christ. The net result of the nearly exclusive and militant concentration on these themes in theologizing and in mass teaching and of the exclusion of the advocacy of the social dimensions of faith, was a set of doctrinal innovations and emphases constituting a variant or a modification of the historical faith instead of apostolic or reformational orthodoxy itself. The labeling of conservatives as Fundamentalists was, then, an accurate indication of this inner transformation of nineteenth-century Evangelicalism.

Thus, not only did the liberals reconstruct their belief system during this period, but the majority of conservatives did so as well, though in perhaps less drastic ways.[7] From this period on, one can only truly understand these two major factions of American Protestantism in their respective relations to modernity. On the one hand, the liberalizing forces in Protestantism must be seen as a direct response—adaptation—to the cognitive pressures posed by modern institutional processes. On the other hand, the very character of Fundamentalism must be regarded at this time as the result of the protest and defense against the world view of modernity in what was considered its most seductive and pernicious expression: modernism.

The Entrenchment of Fundamentalism as a Cognitive Minority, 1919–1942

The processes that had begun before the turn of the century culminated in the decade of the 1920s in what is now remembered as the Fundamentalist–

Modernist controversy.[8] Once again it was a controversy fought not between denominations but within them—Baptist and Presbyterian most notably (Marsden, 1980:192 f.). The issues had already been defined. The Fundamentalists considered the liberals, or Modernists, heretical in their theological orientation. They had abandoned the core of the true Christian faith and replaced it with an adulterated version, one informed by new scientific discoveries and hypotheses (evolution in particular), new methodologies (higher criticism), and the new reductionist interpretations of religious reality (the psychology and sociology of religion). The other side caricatured the Fundamentalists as rude, anti-intellectual, and obscurantist in their theological orientation and presentation. They were thought to be defending an antiquated interpretation of the Bible and religious experience on the basis of noisy dogma, not sound reasoning.

A major event signaling the formal beginning of the controversy was the establishment of the World's Christian Fundamentals Association (WCFA) in the summer of 1919. The organization, made up primarily of millenarian dispensationalists of the urban Northeast, was committed to preserving the great truths of the faith, for as they put it, the "Great Apostasy was spreading like a plague throughout Christendom" (Sandeen, 1970b:243). As such, they also vigorously denounced the FCC, evolution, and anything else that hinted of Modernism. The WCFA started out with tremendous enthusiasm and anticipation of success. Its influence was especially great in the South, for the views promulgated by the WCFA were compatible with the preexisting southern conservatism, individualism, and biblicism. Though its influence in broadcasting Fundamentalist perspectives and solidifying Fundamentalist support was significant at first, as an organization, it soon began to falter. The tenor of the organization in its structure and pronouncements was decisively separatist and sectarian. Within a few short years, the organization collapsed for lack of popular support.

Another central event in the Fundamentalist controversy was the sermon of Harry Emerson Fosdick entitled "Shall the Fundamentalists Win?" This sermon became perhaps the most well known of an increasing number of diatribes against Fundamentalism and served to unite the Modernists against the Fundamentalist protest. Fosdick's sermon had particular reverberations in the Presbyterian denomination, not only in the ecclesiastical hierarchy but in the seminary as well. The major issue for church authorities during the early 1920s was how to deal with the growing number of liberally swayed theologians and ministers. Though initially the policy was to require them to conform to the traditional Calvinist doctrines or else face church discipline, pressure to adopt a position of ecclesiastic and theological tolerance for the liberals was mounting. J. Grescham Machen, one of the leaders of the conservatives from Princeton Seminary, defined the situation as a contest between two logically incompatible religions within denominations and suggested that the liberals leave. Just the opposite occurred. Church authorities adopted a policy of in-house tolerance, and in reaction, the conservatives, led by Machen, initiated a break. The result was a formal split in the Presbyterian denomination aptly symbolized by the establishment of Westminster Theological Seminary in Philadelphia. Similar though less significant patterns of struggle occurred in the Methodist, Episcopal, and Church of Christ denominations, especially in the North (Marsden, 1980:178).

Another front in the controversy was in the sphere of missions. Geographically isolated from the "contaminating" effects of Modernism, the mission field was still largely dominated by conservative forces through the turn of the century. By the 1920s, however, the liberalizing forces in Protestantism had begun to make a showing. As expected, conflict ensued.

A final source of controversy, which had its greatest impact outside of Protestantism proper and in the general culture, was the rising popular acceptance of what were considered non-Christian beliefs. The most tenable and pernicious was thought to be Darwin's theory of evolution and its teaching in the public schools. Between 1921 and 1929, thirty-seven anti-evolution bills, all supported by the Fundamentalist contingent, were introduced into twenty state legislatures (Sandeen, 1970b:226). Yet the most immodest and disreputable of Fundamentalist antievolution initiatives was the highly publicized Scopes trial in 1925. Two prominent lawyers, Clarence Darrow and William Jennings Bryan, faced each other in a legal dispute over Tennessee's antievolution laws and the constitutional rights of a public school teacher, John Scopes, to teach evolution in spite of them. The outcome is well known. Bryan, arguing for the Fundamentalists and against Scopes, won the legal case. Public opinion, however, was clearly in favor of Darrow, who had made mocking sport of the Fundamentalist's crusade. In the end, Fundamentalism was only discredited by the event.

The only issue on which there was agreement between the Fundamentalists and the Modernists was the issue of Prohibition. After years of frustrated attempts, a united coalition of Fundamentalists and Modernists succeeded in passing the Volstead Act and the Eighteenth Amendment to the Constitution—legislation prohibiting the sale of alcohol.

The many events of the Fundamentalist–Modernist controversy marked a culmination in the tensions within Protestantism that had existed for the preceding three decades. Parallel with the general unpopularity of the Protestant-initiated temperance movement, which had reached its peak with Prohibition, the prestige of American Protestantism in general had fallen to unprecedented depths by the 1920s. Protestantism had succumbed to such indecencies as name-calling and backbiting. Indeed, the chief preoccupation within Protestantism during this period was the waging of a sort of in-house civil war. Though the idea of a Protestant empire had not been entirely lost, its active pursuit by Protestantism in general had been abandoned. The revocation of the Volstead Act in 1933 and the drastic decline of foreign missions signaled the end of this empire building.

The events of the 1920s also marked an overall decline in the plausibility of the Protestant world view for the man on the street. A process that had begun in intellectual circles and among church leaders and the clergy had, by this time, percolated down to the level of everyday life. Increasing numbers consciously repudiated the beliefs of conservative Protestantism in favor of the new liberalism. Significant numbers repudiated Christianity in general. In the course of roughly thirty-five years, Protestantism had moved from a position of cultural dominance to a position of cognitive marginality and political impotence. The world view of modernity had gained preponderance in the culture.

A significant event of the 1920s that further mitigated the plausibility of the traditional Protestant world view for the common man was, as Bell (1976) put it, the "invention of mass-consumption." As I have mentioned, a central ornament of the nineteenth-century world view was an ethical system that esteemed the personal virtues of industry, thrift, discipline, and sobriety and eschewed the personal vices of sumptuary excess, indolence, unruliness, and indulgence. Mass consumption is of course predicated on the mass production brought about by technological innovations in the economy. What justified mass consumption in the culture was the discovery of instant credit.

> The greatest single engine in the destruction of the Protestant ethic was the invention of the installment plan, or instant credit. Previously one had to save in order to buy. But with credit cards one could indulge in instant gratification. . . . The Protestant ethic had served to limit sumptuary (though not capital) accumulation. When the Protestant ethic was sundered from bourgeois society, only the hedonism remained, and the capitalist system lost its transcendental ethic. (Bell, 1976:21)

Installment buying, as Bell later pointed out, allayed the old Protestant fear of debt. Through the turn of the century, temperance remained the abiding symbol of the Protestant ethic in America. The revocation of laws of prohibition symbolized its final dissolution as a unifying life ethic in the culture.

Thus, on virtually all fronts Protestantism as a whole suffered a loss of prestige and plausibility. Yet the situation was much more disquieting for the Fundamentalists than for the liberals. This was primarily due to their intransigence on the issue of the nature and place of the supernatural. A world view whose dominant interpretive characteristic was the immediacy of the spiritual in everyday life could now only evoke curiosity as a bewildering oddity. Another important reason for the extreme dislocation of Fundamentalists in the culture was the uninhibited brashness of their social demeanor and the aggressive bellicosity with which they proffered or defended their beliefs. They clearly resented the now-dominant influence of the modern world view in America. The pervasive pessimism of premillennialism only contributed to this attitude. Indeed the Fundamentalists were convinced that the emerging modern world view signaled the inevitable downfall of human thinking and was a veritable sign of the imminence of the Second Coming of Christ. By the end of the 1920s the conservative Protestant conflict with the world view of modernity, initially represented by Modernism and later by the modern (secular) scientific enterprise (with evolution as its symbol) was essentially decided. The stage for the next several decades had been set. Fundamentalism, which had derived its unique identity from this conflict, had lost in its effort to maintain dominance within the denominations and within the general culture, and this resulted in the further loss of credibility of the conservative Protestant meaning system as well as the tarnishing of its collective identity. In the coming years Fundamentalism would have to cope with the pejorative stereotype established in the media during the Scopes trial. After the 1920s, Fundamentalism would remain, in the mind of the man on the street and as a facet of the cultural imagination, a sectarian fringe of American Protestantism.

Corresponding to the colossal economic depression there was, as Marty (1970) and others (Handy, 1971) have noted, a spiritual depression in the culture. Protestantism was particularly affected. What actually seems to be the case is that Protestantism simply continued in the spiritual decline that had characterized previous decades. The difference was that this period was much quieter than previous ones. What is unusual is that under conditions of extreme economic and social deprivation one typically anticipates a forceful resurgence of religious commitment. Indeed some church leaders of the time hailed the collapse of the economy for precisely this reason. The hardship men experienced would drive them back to God, and the church would once again thrive. Although world war and economic depression fostered a general conservatism (in theology the result was neoorthodoxy), a large-scale revival of religion in the culture never came about.[9] Signs of renewal were periodic and relatively unpredictable. Commenting on this state of affairs, Handy (1971) wrote:

> Revival in the old pattern simply did not materialize. Revivalism as it had been developed through the nineteenth and into the twentieth centuries had been in the context of a civilization understood to be Protestant in a general sense. Much of its power was drawn in fact from its community nature and from its confident assumption that in calling men to God it also enlisted them directly in the forces which strengthen the Christian character of a civilization. To answer the call was important, therefore, both for the individual and for society. (p. 208)

Revival had previously been facilitated by the close association that existed between religion (Protestantism) and the rest of society, but the modern processes of institutional differentiation and segmentation slowly severed that institutional association. In response to the pressures brought about by these institutional changes, the quest to establish a Christian America had been abandoned. The sacred covenant had been broken. Religion had been sequestered and formally placed in a contractual relation to society; it was to perform institutionally specific duties. As such, religious renewal in the general culture would be much more difficult. Religion was becoming a private matter, and therefore, were religious renewal to occur, it would have little if any institutional support.

In this situation Fundamentalism, now concentrated in the lower and lower middle classes of the rural and newly industrial South, did not remain dormant but became increasingly entrenched as a cognitive minority. The frustration and dissatisfaction among conservative Presbyterians that ended in the split in Presbyterianism in 1929 foreshadowed the dominant trend in Fundamentalism during the 1930s: the independent church movement (Gaspar, 1963:21–22). The choice was between remaining in what were considered apostate denominations where maintaining a strict orthodoxy would be difficult and withdrawing from those denominations and becoming independent. Cognitive purity is always easier if shielded from contaminating forces, a fact Fundamentalism readily acknowledges in history. The Bible Presbyterian Church, the Bible Protestant Church, the Independent Fundamentalist Churches of America (drawing from several denominations), and many smaller independent churches that remained unaffiliated all emerged during this period. Holiness, Pentecostal, and Adventist groups also proliferated (Jones, 1974). Many smaller conservative (confessional) denominations were also drawn to Fundamentalist principles at this time; the Evangelical Free Church, the Missouri Synod Lutheran, and the Christian Reformed being among the most important (Rudnick, 1966). Denominations in the Anabaptist tradition responded positively as well; here one may mention the Evangelical Mennonites and the Evangelical Friends (Marsden, 1980:195). These groups, in addition to a strong cohort of Baptist and Methodist churches, constituted the major institutional base of Fundamentalism at this time.

In the context of the depression, Fundamentalism, among religious groups, suffered least. The pessimism of Fundamentalist premillennial eschatology was entirely complementary with the socioeconomic conditions Fundamentalists experienced in everyday life. The Great Depression was in their view a sign of God's vindictive punishment on an apostate America as well as a sign of Christ's imminent return. Their nearly exclusive orientation toward spiritual salvation proved adaptive to the deprivation they experienced as well. Personal salvation and the variable degrees of holiness attainable by the believer served as compensations for the privileges denied him in the social and economic spheres.[10]

As suggested, religion in general was being relegated to the private sphere. In the 1920s, the Lynds, in their study *Middletown* (Lynd and Lynd, 1929), remarked: "In theory, religious beliefs dominate all other activities in Middletown; actually, large regions of Middletown's life appear uncontrolled by them" (p. 4). Eight years later, in *Middletown in Transition* (1937), they observed that the gap had grown even wider: religious thought and practice were, in the minds of citizens, increasingly unrelated to other spheres of life:

> The gap between religion's verbalizing and Middletown life has become so wide that the entire institution of religion has tended to be put on the defensive; and the acceptance of a defensive role has tended to mean that it is timid in jeopardizing its foothold in the culture by espousing unpopular causes, when they appear in the economic order, in questions of world peace, and in the elements of contradiction in local institutions. (p. 311)

The pressures of privatization were similar within Fundamentalism. Revivals remained the staple of the Fundamentalist churches. Next in importance to "being saved" was the quest to conform to a rigorous private-sphere morality exclusively oriented around avoiding the sins of worldly amusements: playing cards, dancing, gambling, drinking, going to the movies, and swimming with members of the opposite sex. Conformity to these strictures not only differentiated the Fundamentalist from "the world" (viz., the modern world) in his own mind but provided evidence of his salvation to others in the community.[11] The orientation of this ethic attests to the reality that the Fundamentalist's experience in the church bore little relevance to his experience in the world of work. It also points out the fact that, in these circles, economic prosperity and other forms of public-sphere success were no longer the main indexes of divine favor they had been to the colonial-Puritan and nineteenth-century Evangelicals.

At the same time, there is evidence that suggests that Fundamentalists resisted the pressures of privatization in the political sphere in particular. They were, to be sure, the last remnants of nineteenth-century Evangelicalism to interpret American history in terms of a nation in a covenant with God. Revivalist Billy Sunday in his final years continued to speak for Fundamentalism on the platform, publicly defending the American way of life. To him (and most other Fundamentalists), it meant the patriotic adherence to the ideals of the Republican party and nineteenth-century laissez-faire capitalism and a repudiation of communism (found in the New Deal, the American Civil Liberties Union, and the Democratic party), atheism (evolutionism), and modernism (the FCC, the social gospel, etc.). The opinion was widely held that, if certain trends were not reversed by virtue of a sweeping revival, the world would surely meet destruction. Though rarely, if ever, organized into a viable political force during the 1930s, the Fundamentalist contingent was, nonetheless, seldom ambivalent or silent about its political views on current events and trends in the world.

Recognizing that collective survival depended on an organizational unity, Fundamentalists came together in the fall of 1941 and established the American Council of Christian Churches (ACCC). The council was a logical culmination of the independent church movement, an organization parallel to the FCC, which now represented what was considered mainstream Protestantism. As such, it was designed to bear witness to "the historical faith of the church," including:

> the full truthfulness, inerrancy, and authority of the Bible, which is the Word of God; the holiness and love of the one sovereign God, Father, Son and Holy Spirit; the true deity and sinless humanity of our Lord Jesus Christ, His virgin birth, His atoning death, "the just for the unjust," His bodily resurrection, His glorious coming again; salvation by grace through faith alone; the oneness in Christ of those He had redeemed with His own precious blood; and the maintenance in the visible church of purity of life and doctrine. (Gaspar, 1963:23)

It also was explicitly designed to be a separatist organization for churches or denominations that had denounced modernism and had disavowed affiliation with the FCC "in the darkening days of apostasy." Thus, Fundamentalism was still defining itself formally in reaction to modernity; in protest against the dominance of the modern world view.

Neo-Evangelicalism and the Reconstruction of Conservative Protestantism, 1942–1980

Soon after the establishment of the ACCC, a group of moderate Fundamentalists came together to explore the possibilities of establishing another national Protestant organization that "was determined to break with apostasy," as the ACCC had been, but that would be "no dog-in-the-manger, reactionary, negative or destructive type of organization." It would also "shun all forms of bigotry, intolerance, misrepresentation, hate, jealousy, false judgment and hypocrisy" (Murch, 1952). In the spring of 1942 the National Association of Evangelicals (NAE) was formally constituted.[12] There was complete unity between the ACCC and the NAE in matters of doctrine, but they differed in matters of policy. Membership in the former was exclusive, no members of the FCC being allowed to participate; membership in the latter was more inclusive, selective membership for the affiliates of the FCC being permitted. These membership policies are suggestive of an overall difference of attitude between the two theologically conservative groups. Where the former held a rigid "no cooperation, no compromise" attitude toward differing theological traditions, the latter held the more conciliatory attitude, "cooperation without compromise." Indeed, these attitudes applied also to their respective approaches to the dominant culture in general. Though the two groups often shared intemperate hostility toward one another as a result of these policy differences, together they constituted the dual alignment of conservative Protestantism in America for the next three decades.

The postwar period of the 1950s and 1960s was, without question, the most economically opulent in American history. The exterior appearance of a pseudoaristocracy was obtainable for an increasing number of Americans, and a brash materialism came to dominate life in the private sphere. A respectable hedonism made possible by the postwar economic growth was institutionalized as a normative expectation in the mainstream of the culture. Through this period and in this context, a general religious renewal took place. Church membership in the United States grew from 43 percent in 1920, to 47 percent in 1930, to 49 percent in 1940, to 57 percent in 1950, to 62 percent in 1956, and to 63 percent in the early 1960s (Marty, 1970:258; cf. Herberg, 1955). As Marty (1970) notes:

> After the American religious depression of the 1930s and the preoccupations of World War II, it became clear that by around 1950 many Americans were in a settling-down mood. They needed a means of justifying their complacencies, soothing their anxieties, pronouncing benedictions on their way of life, and organizing the reality around them. Millions turned to religion, and Protestantism profited from the return to religion. (p. 256)

The greatest preoccupation of mainstream Protestantism during this time was coping with modern religious pluralism.[13] Since 1908, when the ecumenical FCC had been formed, little had been accomplished in unifying Christianity, yet cultural pluralism had become even more commonplace and demanded to be addressed by the ecclesiastical structure. In 1948 the international ecumenical movement gained impetus with the founding of the World Council of Churches (WCC). In two years the FCC was reconstituted into a more ecumenical structure in the founding of the National Council of Churches of Christ in the United States (NCC). Both organizations sought to go beyond Protestantism to include in membership Eastern Orthodoxy and even Roman Catholicism. Thus, the pluralist interpretation of American life, where all religious traditions stood on equal ground, was finally becoming established in the mainstream of American culture. Interreligious "dialogue" (a religious détente) became the fashion of the day. The ideological justification (as in 1908) was the unity of God's church for the ultimate goal of establishing God's kingdom on earth through progressive social policies. Clearly more was at stake. The aggressive ecumenism of mainstream Protestantism not only marked a continued yielding to the cognitive constraints of modern cultural pluralism but implied a recognition of the market character of religions in competition for the "interest, allegiance and financial support of potential clientele." Ecumenicity rationalizes and civilizes competition as does the process of cartelization in the secular economy (P. Berger, 1963:85).

In the late 1950s and early 1960s there remained an optimism about the social and political efficacy of the church in a world beset by acute needs. Ecumenicity had caught hold in Roman Catholicism under Pope John, signaling progress toward unity between Protestantism and Catholicism in their efforts to establish the kingdom of God on earth. The optimism in mainstream Protestantism was also sustained by the continued influx of liberal Protestant churchgoers. Liberal Protestant theology was meanwhile undergoing drastic changes. Theological notions such as the "death of God" and the "secular city" as the workshop of God became very popular. The gospel message and the identity and role of the church were to be redefined in secular, humanistic terms. True spirituality was defined as the forthright accommodation to the world view and life patterns of modernity. Yet the theological innovations of the early 1960s turned out to be little more than the further cognitive contamination that accompanies dialogue with different religious traditions and with the naturalism of the modern world view. The world view of mainstream Protestantism and liberal theology by the middle of the decade could well be described as the forthright religious legitimation of modernity.

Conservative Protestantism also fared well in the postwar social and political atmosphere of conservatism. Its organizations became more cohesive, and its policies became more deliberate. The Fundamentalists and neo-Evangelicals reacted sharply to the ecumenical initiatives of mainstream Protestantism (Gaspar, 1963:40–74). Most of all they feared the rise of a superchurch that, as the Bible prophesied, would be established in the last days. The ecumenical movement and its many organizations were, they believed, the precursors of this universal church. Their criticism was, as expected, unrelenting; but their reaction went beyond words. Several days before the constituent assembly of the WCC in 1948, Carl McIntire, president of the ACCC, assembled a delegation of Fundamentalists in the same city and established the International Council of Christian Churches (ICCC) as a counterorganization to the WCC. McIntire took full advantage of the resulting media event to publicize the Fundamentalist grievances with liberal Protestantism. Similar acts were repeated through the 1950s whenever the WCC or its constituent national councils met.

The greatest militancy of Fundamentalism during this period was directed toward the anticommunist crusade.[14] The national sentiment was decidedly conservative on this issue, largely because of the unsettling nature of the Soviet initiatives in Eastern Europe (the cold war) and the swelling nationalism in Asia. The notion of an internal conspiracy designed to subvert governments to communism could seem plausible in this setting and thereby provide a climate favorable to the cultivation of anticommunist programs. Fundamentalists McIntire of the ACCC-ICCC, Edgar Bundy of the Church League of America, and Billy James Hargis of the Christian Crusade all came to the fore in the anticommunist operations of the early 1950s. The relationship between the two movements was, to be sure, symbiotic. Of particular concern to the Fundamentalists was the infiltration of communism into the church, so they centered their attacks on the NCC and the WCC as apostate, un-American, procommunist, and treasonous ecclesiastical organizations. The formula was simple: liberalism is socialism, and socialism is the first phase of communism. On several occasions throughout this period, the Fundamentalists held McCarthy-style exposés of prominent WCC and NCC leaders to attempt to substantiate their allegations.

The more moderate neo-Evangelicals, though generally supportive of the efforts of the Fundamentalists, were sharply critical of the manner in which many of the latter's activities were carried out and therefore avoided direct involvement. The neo-Evangelicals channeled most of their energies into the reconstruction of a strong subcultural infrastructure (Gaspar, 1963:93–147). Most basic was their effort to reestablish a stable foundation of popular support through evangelism. Religious radio programs such as the "Back to the Bible Hour," "The Children's Gospel Hour," "The Hour of Decision," "Radio Bible Class," "Old Fashioned Revival Hour," and religious radio stations such as WMBI, KUCA, KUGA, and WMUU proliferated in the postwar period.[15] Evangelical television programming also got its start at this time with "Youth on the March," "Sermons from Science," and "Man to Man." Youth evangelistic organizations such as Youth for Christ, the Miracle Book Club, the American Soul Clinic, Inter-Varsity Christian Fellowship, and others providing alternative forms of teenage entertainment also became popular at this time. All of these efforts met with shocking success. Providing the most forceful influence, however, was the evangelistic fervor of mass evangelist Billy Graham. His crusades held in Los Angeles, Portland, Boston, Columbia, South Carolina, and New York between 1949 and 1957 were overwhelmingly successful, not only in "saving souls" but in making the premillennialist Evangelical world view palatable in the mainstream of American culture again.

Neo-Evangelicalism exhibited positive growth in other areas as well. With the establishment of the NAE came the formal involvement of many of the conservative denominations in the Reformed-Confessional tradition. Thus, Evangelicalism gained denominational strength. In addition, Bible institutes, Evangelical liberal arts colleges, and Evangelical seminaries emerged concomitant with the need to educate the increasing numbers of new adherents. During the postwar period through the 1950s the Christian day school movement surfaced as an alternative to primary and secondary public education. The movement gained notable momentum when the legislative efforts to provide for "released-time" religious education in the public schools (permitting students to voluntarily receive religious education during school hours on school property) were defeated.

Quite naturally, substantial growth in Evangelical scholarship also occurred. After the 1920s few if any conservative Protestant thinkers in America were taken seriously in intellectual circles. After World War II great efforts were made to reverse this trend. Anti-intellectualism was repudiated in favor of a scholastic attitude dedicated to preserving the essentials of Evangelical orthodoxy on thoroughly rational grounds. Thus, neo-Evangelical scholars attempted to deal with modern rational thought on its own terms. Evangelical apologetics became the main intellectual activity, and in the process, certain concessions were made.[16] Neo-Evangelical scholars also began to become sensitive to the social import of their faith. Slowly there arose formal efforts at developing direction for Evangelical social thought. As a result of many of these "clarifications" and of the promise that the doctrines of Evangelicalism could be rationally defended if necessary, the religious orientation of Evangelicalism gained a measure of credibility in the culture.

Finally, periodicals emerged to serve the expanding community of educated Evangelicals. *Christianity Today, Eternity, Youth for Christ Magazine, His,* and *Christian Life* are examples of these, as are more scholarly journals such as *Journal of the Evangelical Theological Society, Gordon Review,* and the *Journal of the American Scientific Affiliation.* Evangelical publishing houses profited from this expansion as well, as their growth in number and in size of operation shows.

Thus, in virtually all ways, were the neo-Evangelicals, now simply called Evangelicals, successful in their construction of a firm subcultural foundation. Applying the interpretive framework of this research, one can say that the Evangelicals had established lines of cognitive defense from which to withstand the cognitive onslaught of modernity and within which the meaning system of conservative Protestantism could be plausibly maintained. More than that, conservative Protestantism in Evangelicalism had by the end of the 1950s clearly outgrown its insecurities as a cognitive minority. Indeed, it had successfully shed the stigma of being a religious sect and had come to enjoy a central place within the mainstream of American culture. Nothing better illustrated this success than the celebrity status accorded Billy Graham.

The trends established within conservative Protestantism in the 1950s continued through the 1960s and beyond. Widely discredited by its association with McCarthyism, Fundamentalism continued its hard-sell campaign against liberal theology, ecumenicism, and communism. This along with revivalism constituted its exclusive orientation, and thus Fundamentalism continued to appeal to the rural lower classes. Evangelicalism, on the other hand, continued its general policy of extending its popular and institutional base of support as well as its influence in American society (Sandeen, 1970a). Evangelicals maintained their alliance with political conservatism, as evidenced by their support of the Goldwater presidential campaign in 1964, the close association of Billy Graham with higher echelons of political power, their struggle to reinstitute prayer and Bible reading in the public schools, their lack of support of the civil rights movement, and their general support of the American involvement in the war in Southeast Asia. The one exception to this was the much-publicized "Evangelical hippies," or "Jesus people," factions of whom were far from being exclusively pietistic. These maintained, as their secular counterparts did, a fairly well-defined, left-liberal political orientation (J. D. Hunter, 1980b).

From the end of the 1960s to the present, mainstream Protestantism has remained ecclesiastically stable and theologically more subdued; yet to the delight of conservatives, it has experienced a radical decline in popular support. Membership in and attendance at the mainstream churches have dwindled. The world view of mainstream Protestantism has, from all indications, been showing signs of cognitive impotency in the culture. Conservative Protestantism, on the other hand, has continued to build strong and stable institutions. Evangelicalism, having maintained equilibrium through the 1960s, showed clear signs of a resurgence by the early 1970s (Bloesch, 1973). Beginning with the rise of the Jesus people in the last years of the Vietnam war, the resurgence peaked in 1976 with the media spectacle of the born-again movement, the election of Evangelical Jimmy Carter to the presidency, and the designation of the national bicentennial as the Year of the Evangelical. Whereas through the previous two decades conservative Protestantism had maintained a relatively low profile, it had by 1976 become the object of public attention. Suddenly, it was acceptable and even socially desirable to become a born-again Christian. Celebrities such as President Nixon's former aide Charles Colson, rock star Eric Clapton, pornographer Larry Flynt, and political expatriate Eldridge Cleaver were making headlines with their conversion experiences. Within Evangelicalism confidence had grown to such an extent by the mid-1970s that Evangelical leaders such as Bill Bright could boldly predict the evangelization of the United States by 1980 and the total evangelization of the world by 1984.

Whether the resurgence of Evangelicalism in the 1970s was a genuine religious revival or simply a media-encouraged (or media-constructed) revival, it is difficult to say. There was a significant stirring within conservative Protestantism that began to subside only toward the end of the decade. Throughout this resurgence and up to this writing, Evangelicalism continued to maintain its close association with "middle-brow" American culture, as it had from the 1950s. Normally, this has meant the quiet affirmation of everyday American middle-class life patterns—in extreme cases, the aping of the glitter and pageantry of Hollywood (Bloesch, 1973:24 f.; J. Johnson, 1980; Quebedeaux, 1978).

Of special significance is the dissolution of the distinction between Fundamentalism and Evangelicalism as a result of the Evangelical resurgence.

This is not to say that there is no longer any diversity along these lines among conservative Protestants. Clearly conservative Protestantism has always been and remains a polymorphic and heterogeneous group, not only in the religious dimensions but in the structural and cultural dimensions as well. What is different as a result of the Evangelical resurgence is that the policy differences that precipitated the bifurcation in Fundamentalism in the 1940s are no longer rigidly institutionalized. Although there are clear remnants of the "1920s Fundamentalism" still to be found within conservative Protestantism (the ACCC and ICCC, Bob Jones University, and Hargis and his Christian Crusade), they no longer make up the formidable cultural and political force they once did. By and large this militant faction of the tradition has been brought into mainline Evangelicalism,[17] which may be largely due to the reality-defining capacities of the media, specifically through their labeling of all conservative Protestants as Evangelicals.

Perhaps the best description of American Evangelicalism during the period between 1943 and 1982 is offered by Marty: Evangelicalism has remained a cognitive minority but has emerged as a sociocultural majority. The core elements of the Evangelical meaning system remain as they were in the beginning of the century. Along with the standard tenets of Christian orthodoxy (the trinitarian nature of God, etc.), these are the centrality of the Bible as the infallible and inerrant Word of God, the deity and historicity of Jesus Christ and the essentiality of establishing and maintaining a personal relationship with Jesus Christ for one's salvation. Following from this is the belief in the necessity of the proselytization of all humankind for Christianity (which typically means Evangelicalism); the belief in the personal (typically premillennial) Second Coming of Christ; and the individuated conception of personal, social, and institutional problems (i.e., the sinful heart and mind of the individual as the root cause and explanation of all human ills). On these beliefs Evangelicals are, in the main, intransigent. Consequently, in a broader social world where the secular is defined as normative, such specific and exclusivistic beliefs must at the least be considered tolerably deviant, if not intolerably divisive. At the same time the sociocultural genre of contemporary Evangelicalism is firmly representative of the world of the American middle class, who are dominant in American society. In this situation Evangelicalism can demonstrate widespread public acceptance. How can this be possible?

One could hypothesize that some concessions have been made with modernity. With the growing plausibility of the modern world view resulting from the extension of the modernization processes in American society, came the increased pressure to accommodate. The establishment of the NAE marks the point in the history of American conservative Protestantism at which a yielding to those pressures began—the point at which a more positive and constructive, or perhaps a more conciliatory, approach to modernity was taken. In the most general terms, one can understand the efforts to develop a rational apologetic for Protestant orthodoxy and the efforts to establish stable institutional structures within the Evangelical community as dimensions in which this trend can be seen. One can understand Evangelicals embracing modern technology and modern (middle-class) forms of cultural expression in the same way. Thus, the Evangelicals have been successful at establishing lines of cognitive defense, but not without some sacrifice.

This conciliatory approach to modernity may be seen in more subtle terms as well. From its earliest times, Fundamentalism (as a variant of nineteenth-century Evangelical Protestantism) defined itself in opposition to the world view of modernity as it found expression in theological Modernism. The presuppositions and concepts of the modern world view were understood to be sinful, and its emerging predominance in the culture was seen as a sign of the end of human history. Being distinct from the world (viz., the modern world) was thus very important for the Fundamentalists; it remains important in conservative Protestant circles. Yet until the early 1940s this separatism was defined exclusively in negative terms; in other words, the world view of modernity is utterly sinful, so it should be abhorred and avoided at all costs. After this point, however, there emerged a growing trend toward defining separatism more positively; in other words, the world view of modernity is sinful, so one must prove at all costs the superiority of Evangelicalism. This latter approach has required greater involvement of Evangelicals with the modern society in which they find themselves, an involvement that has had important implications for the character and vitality of the Evangelical world view.

This attempt to interpret historically the general patterns of relation between modernity (ipso facto, the world view of modernity) and the meaning system of American conservative Protestantism is necessary to the paramount task of this research: the untangling of the complexities of present-day Evangelicalism. But before pursuing these issues more diligently, it is appropriate to explore with greater care the question Who are the contemporary American Evangelicals?

4

A Demographic Profile

A recent public opinion survey of the general American population (see Appendix 2) revealed that roughly 22 percent of, or more than one of every five, Americans (two of every five Protestants) 18 years of age and older are Evangelicals (see Appendix 1). A group of this size, it would seem, could command the focused attention of some social scientists; yet this has not been the case. Until recently, very little has been known about contemporary American Evangelicals, especially their demographic characteristics. Most discussion of that dimension rests therefore on vague impressions and inherited historical stereotypes and yields ambiguous results. Although such impressions and stereotypes might prove true in the end, it is important to examine them for any grounding they may have in empirical data and to qualify or reject them accordingly. I pursue this kind of analysis of American Evangelical demographics in comparison with other religious or purportedly nonreligious groups: liberal (non-Evangelical) Protestants, who make up roughly 35 percent of the general American population; Catholics, who are around 30 percent; non-Christians (Jews and others), who are approximately 4 percent; and secularists (those with no religious preference), who are around 9 percent.

Background Demographics

A good starting point is the ascriptive demographic characteristics of the population: race, gender, age, and marital status (see Table 4.1). A 10-to-1 ratio (90.4 to 8.9%) of whites to blacks in the general population closely parallels that in the Evangelical community (88.2 to 11.8%). The percentage difference is even lower among Protestant liberals and secularists. Among Catholics and non-Christians, the percentage difference is significantly greater. Although a low percentage of blacks is not any surprise in the Catholic and non-Christian categories, the percentage of Evangelical blacks is lower

49

TABLE 4.1

BACKGROUND BY RELIGIOUS PREFERENCE (in percentages)

Race	Evangelical	Liberal	Catholic	Non-Christian	Secularist
White	88.2	87.2	97.7	96.4	87.6
Black	11.8	12.8	2.3	3.6	12.4
	100.0	100.0	100.0	100.0	100.0
Gender					
Male	40.1	51.7	45.1	53.6	63.4
Female	59.9	48.3	54.9	46.4	36.6
	100.0	100.0	100.0	100.0	100.0
Age					
18–35	27.1	37.9	43.1	46.4	66.9
36–50	26.5	22.2	24.5	21.4	16.2
51–65	24.8	22.1	20.0	14.3	12.3
66 up	21.6	17.8	12.4	17.9	4.6
	100.0	100.0	100.0	100.0	100.0
(Average age)	(48.4)	(45.4)	(41.7)	(43.7)	(34.3)
Marital status					
Married	77.2	72.8	69.0	57.2	57.6
Single	7.8	12.2	19.0	26.8	28.0
Separated or divorced	4.9	5.4	4.6	7.1	11.4
Widowed	10.1	9.6	7.4	8.9	3.0
	100.0	100.0	100.0	100.0	100.0
N =	(347)	(540)	(474)	(56)	(132)

than might be expected. Black religion has always been thought of as a "religion of the disinherited"—oriented toward salvation, revival, holiness, and biblical literalism—in a word, crudely Evangelical. Yet current data do not support this idea. Evangelical and mainstream Protestants each have roughly the same percentage of blacks.

The gender characteristics of the Evangelical subculture are notable as well. In the general population there are roughly equal numbers of men and women (48.1 and 51.9%, respectively). Yet in the sample of Evangelicals, there was a significantly greater (20% greater) percentage of women than men. The differential was only greater among the secularists, where it was over 25 percent, and in this case the percentage of men exceeded that of women. Among liberal Protestants, Catholics, and non-Christians, there was a general parity with the national breakdown (though less so among Catholics). The two extremes taken along with the example of Catholicism provide initial verification of the commonplace in the sociology of religion that women are more likely to be affiliated with a conservative religious body than are men in modern societies—an issue I explore more fully later.

Age is another dimension of interest. With the average age of all the respondents at 43.9 years, Evangelicals display an older population, with a mean of 48.4 years. Once again at the other extreme are the secularists, with a mean age of 34.3. Liberal Protestants, Catholics, and non-Christians hover within two years of the total average. Among the Evangelicals there is also a fairly equal distribution between the age categories, whereas the overall tendency is a distinct lowering in percentage the higher in age the respondents are. The greatest drop is between the 18-to-35 and 36-to-50 categories. This tendency is especially sharp among the secularists, less so among non-Christians, and still lesser so among Catholics and liberal Protestants. Without the benefit of a longitudinal study, the data, limited as it is, again generally supports the sociology-of-religion proposition that religious conservatism increases with age.

A final dimension of note is marital status. Among the variety of religious preferences, the greatest percentage of married respondents (77.2%) were Evangelicals, followed in succession by mainstream Protestants, Catholics, secularists, and non-Christians. Evangelicals also showed the lowest percentage of singles (7.8%) and the second-lowest percentage of separated or divorced couples (4.9%) (second to Catholics). As one might expect, the secularists were at the opposite extreme of the continuum.

Thus far one may conclude that although still disproportionately represented within Protestantism, blacks can no longer be seen as exclusively conservative in religious orientation, though black women are more likely to be oriented this way than are black men. Contemporary Evangelicalism is, of course, a white religious phenomenon. Moreover, Evangelicalism shares with Catholicism alone the disproportional percentage of women, though the imbalance is significantly greater in the former than in the latter. Although Evangelicals are strongly represented in the youngest age bracket, the average age (white or black, male or female) is slightly older than that of any other religious tradition. It is especially older than the average age of those with no religious preference. Finally, adult Evangelicals are, more than any other religious type, prone to be married rather than single, maintaining a level of separation and divorce just under the average of the national sample.

Geographics

Another important demographic dimension on which to locate American Evangelicalism is the geographic or regional dimension (see Table 4.2). As one might suspect, the greatest percentage of Evangelicals (45%) are in the South, the region extending from Virginia to Florida and west to Texas and Oklahoma. Two of every five Southerners are Evangelicals. Evangelicals are fairly equally distributed in other regions of the country (ranging between 11.5 and 14.7%), with the exception of New England, where there are only

TABLE 4.2

GEOGRAPHICS BY RELIGIOUS PREFERENCE (in percentages)

Region	Evangelical	Liberal	Catholic	Non-Christian	Secularist
New England	2.0	4.8	8.4	17.9	7.6
Mid-Atlantic	14.1	18.9	29.5	26.8	24.2
East central	14.7	20.9	18.8	8.9	15.9
West central	11.5	10.4	12.7	10.7	6.1
South	45.0	25.7	13.9	14.3	19.7
Rocky Mountain/Pacific	12.7	19.3	16.7	21.4	26.5
	100.0	100.0	100.0	100.0	100.0
City size					
Rural	43.7	33.6	18.0	14.0	22.3
2,500–49,999	19.3	18.3	12.3	14.0	14.9
50,000–999,999	28.4	32.8	33.2	38.0	37.2
1,000,000 and up	8.6	15.3	36.5	34.0	25.6
	100.0	100.0	100.0	100.0	100.0
N =	(347)	(540)	(474)	(56)	(132)

2 percent. Perceived from a slightly different angle—excluding the South; the west central region, where the ratio of Evangelicals to non-Evangelicals is 2 in 10; and New England, where it is less than 1 in 10—the ratio of Evangelicals to non-Evangelicals in the remaining sections of the country is little better than 1 in 10. Liberal Protestants have their greatest showing in the South as well; otherwise they are fairly equally distributed throughout the mid-Atlantic, east central, and Rocky Mountain/Pacific regions. Catholics, as would be expected, are most strongly represented in the mid-Atlantic region, followed in strength by the east central region (Indiana, Illinois, Michigan, and Ohio) and the Rocky Mountain/Pacific region. The weakest showing of Catholics was New England, yet there roughly 43 percent of the population is Catholic. Those with a non-Christian faith are found most significantly in the mid-Atlantic, Rocky Mountain/Pacific region, and the South.

Also interesting is the community size in which the Evangelicals are located. As one might again suspect, Evangelicals are disproportionately (43.7%) represented in rural areas (communities of less than 2,500). The next greatest percentage of Evangelicals is found in the medium-size cities (28.4%), followed by the small towns (population 2,500–50,000) at 19.3 percent. Only 8.6 percent of all Evangelicals surveyed were in cities of one million and more. The pattern of distribution of liberal Protestants crudely mirrors that of Evangelicals but not quite as sharply. Most liberal Protestants are found in rural areas or in medium-size cities. The remainder are fairly equally distributed among large cities and small towns. The distribution of

Catholics is very different; approximately 70 percent of all Catholics reside in medium or large cities, the remainder in the rural areas and small towns. Non-Christians and secularists are also found in the medium and large cities, with dwindling numbers in the small-town and rural areas. The only exception to this is the comparatively sizable percentage of secularists in rural areas.

When examining each group along regional lines but holding community size constant, the situation becomes even more clear (J. D. Hunter, 1980a). Corresponding to the popular conceptions, Evangelicalism is most greatly represented in the rural regions of the small-town southern, west central, and mid-Atlantic states. The liberal Protestants' greatest geographic strength is in the rural, small-town South and the urban mid-Atlantic region; the geographic strength of Catholics is in the urban areas of the mid-Atlantic and east central regions; and the geographic strength of non-Christians is in the urban Northeast and the Rocky Mountain/Pacific region. Finally, the secularists are most concentrated in the urban areas of the mid-Atlantic and Rocky Mountain/Pacific regions.

Social and Economic Demographics

Of utmost importance in understanding the social location of American Evangelicalism are three key variables: income, education, and occupation.[1] On no other topics is there more speculation with as little empirical verification. It is generally held that, as a population, Evangelicals have moved in the past fifty years from the lowest levels of income, education, and occupation to a more middle-echelon position. Yet the data do not entirely confirm this belief.

Evangelicals are typically found in the middle and lower annual household income brackets (see Table 4.3). Of those surveyed, 25.3 percent of Evangelicals were in the lowest income level ($6,999 and under); 37.2 percent are in the $7,000 to $15,000 bracket; 30.4 percent are in the $15,000 to $25,000 bracket; and only 7.1 percent are in the highest income level ($25,000 and up). There are a greater percentage of Evangelicals in the lowest category than in any other religious group, greater also than the national average. Likewise, there are a smaller percentage of Evangelicals, only 7 percent, in the highest income bracket. The bulk of all respondents fell approximately evenly among the two middle-income levels.

Education is another dimension on which it is generally considered that Evangelicals have made positive strides (see Table 4.3). Although this may be true in relation to the national sample and in relation to those of other religious persuasions, the Evangelical population is the only group that exceeds the average of the national sample not completing the eighth grade (8.6%) or high school (28.9%), at the same time falling under the average of

TABLE 4.3

Social Class by Religious Preference (in percentages)

Household income	Evangelical	Liberal	Catholic	Non-Christian	Secularist
$6,999 and under	25.3	23.9	20.4	17.3	16.5
$7,000–$14,999	37.2	32.0	30.5	3.8	37.8
$15,000–$24,999	30.4	27.9	31.0	55.8	29.9
$25,000 and up	7.1	16.2	18.1	23.1	15.8
	100.0	100.0	100.0	100.0	100.0
Education					
Less than 8 years	8.6	4.1	5.2	1.8	3.0
8–11 years	28.9	21.9	19.9	8.9	17.6
High school	38.3	42.2	41.9	21.4	33.6
Some university	15.3	17.4	18.6	25.0	16.0
University	8.9	14.4	14.4	42.9	29.8
	100.0	100.0	100.0	100.0	100.0
Occupation of chief wage earner					
Profession	8.0	17.0	16.5	41.8	27.6
Manager	12.4	12.1	10.0	18.2	4.7
Clerk	6.5	7.9	10.0	5.5	8.7
Skilled worker	30.5	28.0	33.2	12.7	37.8
Laborer	10.9	10.4	12.4	1.8	11.8
Retired	28.7	21.2	15.1	16.4	6.2
Full-time student	0.6	0.9	0.4	3.6	2.4
Housewife	2.4	2.5	2.4	0.0	0.8
	100.0	100.0	100.0	100.0	100.0
Home ownership					
Own	78.0	77.2	69.6	59.3	57.7
Rent	22.0	22.8	30.4	40.7	42.3
	100.0	100.0	100.0	100.0	100.0
N =	(347)	(540)	(474)	(56)	(132)

the national sample of those with high school or trade school educations (38.3%), incomplete university training (15.3%), and complete university educations (8.9%). Liberal Protestants and Catholics closely parallel each other while mirroring the national breakdown. Non-Christians far exceed all other religious bodies in educational achievement, with 68 percent achieving some university training (compared to 24.2% of Evangelicals). Secularists are the only others coming close to this. Although the general pattern of low educational achievement relative to other religious groups remains constant when controlling for age, educational achievement increases among the younger Evangelicals (J. D. Hunter, 1980a).

The greatest percentage of Evangelicals come from families whose chief wage earner has a working-class occupation—the skilled-worker or tradesman and laborer categories, (41.4%) (see Table 4.3). Another 12.4 percent are managers or else own their own small business, and 6.5 percent fall into the lower middle-class, white-collar occupations (sales workers, clerical workers, etc.). In the middle and upper middle-class professions, Evangelicals are, at 8 percent, far underrepresented. This compares to 17 percent of all liberal Protestants, 16.5 percent of all Catholics, 41.8 percent of all non-Christians, and 27.6 percent of all secularists. Evangelicals are overrepresented in the category of those retired. Approximately 29 percent of all Evangelicals are a part of families whose chief wage earner is retired, a percentage significantly greater than that among liberal Protestants, Catholics, non-Christians, or secularists.

Overall, contemporary Evangelicals are most widely represented among the moderately educated, lower and lower middle-income, working-class occupations. There are indications, however, that Evangelicals are rising in these categories owing to a more highly educated younger population. Yet grounding them firmly in the middle, lower middle, and working class is the fact that Evangelical Protestants are more likely than people of any other group to be home owners rather than home renters (see Table 4.3).

In contrast, Catholics and liberal Protestants, though most widely represented in working-class occupations (truer among Catholics than among liberal Protestants), are stronger in the professions and other white-collar occupations than are Evangelicals. They are also typically better educated and more likely to have a greater household income than Evangelical Protestants. Non-Christians are characteristically well educated, of middle and higher household incomes, and found in the professions, management, and as small-business owners. Finally, the secularists are typically professional or skilled workers and tradesmen of middle income with generally higher education. All of this generally confirms the impression of Evangelicalism relative to other religious groups. Evangelicalism remains based within the middle and lower socioeconomic echelons of American life—lower overall than the other major bodies yet clearly not within the lowest reaches of social and economic life.

Political Orientations

During the early 1960s a good deal of research (B. Johnson's, 1962, 1964, is particularly notable) tested the relationship between conservative Protestantism and political party preference. Based on that research, it was generally concluded that there was an unmistakable association between Fundamentalism and Republican party preference—that when liberals and Fundamentalists were compared, Fundamentalists would be more inclined toward Republicanism than would liberals, even when class is controlled. The

sample examined here provides some interesting evidence on political preferences as of 1980 (see Table 4.4). Political party preference among Evangelicals—very different than it was in the early 1960s—is 30.3 percent
Republican, 43 percent Democratic, and 26.7 percent independent. This
compares to 25.9 percent Republican, 44 percent Democratic, and 30.1
percent independent preference among liberal Protestants. While a greater
percentage of Evangelicals than liberal Protestants, Catholics, non-Christians, and secularists are Republicans, the clear majority of Evangelicals are
Democrats. This general pattern of Democratic predominance holds constant
when independently controlling for household income and education at the
lower levels of those categories (i.e., less than a complete high school or
trade school education; less than $15,000 annual income). Yet when con-
trolling for education at the higher levels (combining categories of those
with incomplete and complete university education), there is a reversal, with
the greatest percentage having a Republican party preference. This same
pattern occurred at the higher income levels; there was a higher ratio of
those with Republican party preference among those at the highest income
level (see Table 4.5). Thus it would seem that in 1980 religious preference
has less effect on political party preference (though not necessarily on other
dimensions of political activity) than does social class—a change from the
early 1960s.

Social Organization

As I noted in Chapter 3, Evangelicals have channeled most of their energies
into the construction of a large and stable institutional infrastructure. Sandeen (1970a) remarked on this in his discussion of the tendency of Evangelicalism toward "parallel institutionalism." At the foundation of the social
organization of Evangelicalism is the church; Evangelicals rank higher in
percentage of church members (86%) than any other religious group (see
Table 4.6). Catholics rank next, at 77 percent; and the liberal Protestants
follow at 64.1 percent. The denominational breakdown of the two Protestant parties is interesting (J. D. Hunter, 1980a). Although most strongly
represented among the Baptists, Evangelicals are also strongly represented
among Methodists, Lutherans, and Presbyterians, which is so even among
what are typically considered liberal denominations. Liberal Protestants are
more evenly distributed among the major denominations. What is most obvious from this data is that Evangelicals, although unquestionably a vibrant
force in American Protestantism, still remain a minority position in the
denominations. The only denominations in which Evangelicals are a majority are the Southern Baptist and the small Baptist, Presbyterian, and other
Protestant denominations. In the Missouri Synod Lutheran and in the Disciples of Christ, Evangelicals make up about half the membership. In all

TABLE 4.4

POLITICAL PARTY PREFERENCE BY RELIGIOUS PREFERENCE (in percentages)

	Evangelical	Liberal	Catholic	Non-Christian	Secularist
Republican	30.3	25.9	15.0	10.7	8.5
Democratic	43.0	44.0	53.3	55.4	35.9
Independent	26.7	30.1	31.6	33.9	55.6
	100.0	100.0	100.0	100.0	100.0
N =	(347)	(540)	(474)	(56)	(132)

TABLE 4.5

INCOME AND EDUCATION BY POLITICAL PARTY PREFERENCE,
EVANGELICALS ONLY (in percentages)

Household income	Republican	Democratic	Independent
$6,999 and under	18.2	34.5	20.1
$7,000–$14,999	40.4	36.8	36.0
$15,000–$24,999	32.3	23.7	36.0
$25,000 and up	9.1	5.0	7.9
	100.0	100.0	100.0
Educational achievement			
Less than 8 years	5.9	11.8	6.7
8–11 years	23.5	40.0	17.8
High school	41.2	31.7	44.4
Some university	16.7	11.7	20.0
University	12.7	4.8	11.1
	100.0	100.0	100.0

TABLE 4.6

CHURCH OR SYNAGOGUE MEMBERSHIP BY RELIGIOUS PREFERENCE (in percentages)

	Evangelical	Liberal	Catholic	Non-Christian	Secularist
Yes	86.0	64.1	77.0	46.3	7.7
No	14.0	35.9	23.0	53.7	92.3
	100.0	100.0	100.0	100.0	100.0
N =	(347)	(540)	(474)	(56)	(132)

other major denominations the liberals have the demographic ascendancy.

Outside of the church are the innumerable parallel institutions. Besides the NAE, which operates more or less as an umbrella accrediting agency, Evangelicals have at their disposal over 450 Bible colleges, liberal arts colleges, and seminaries. This is not to mention the thousands of private Evangelical primary and secondary schools that are a part of the National Association of Christian Schools. For virtually every professional and scholarly organization in America, there exists an equivalent—the American Scientific Affiliation, the Christian Association for Psychological Studies, the Christian Medical Association, the Christian Businessman's Association, the Evangelical Press Association, the Christian Veterinarians' Fellowship, and the Fellowship of Christian Athletes, to name a few. There is also a vast structure of Evangelical publishing houses (over 70 in all). Among the largest of these are Word, Inc.; Fleming H. Revell Company; B. Eerdmans Publishing Company; Zondervan Corporation; Moody Press; Tyndale House Publishers; David C. Cook Publishing Company; Baker Book House; Logos International; and Vision House Publishing Company. As one might expect, there are dozens of Evangelical companies producing monthly or bimonthly popular periodicals. There are periodicals such as *Campus Life, Eternity, Moody Monthly, The Evangelical Beacon, Christian Life, Christian Herald, Christian Beacon, The Christian Inquirer, The Christian News, The Christian Digest,* and *Christianity Today.* There are also Evangelical recording companies such as the Maranatha Music Company and the hundreds of Evangelical radio stations that are a part of the International Christian Broadcasters Association. There is even an Evangelical television station—Christian Broadcasting Network (CBN)—which sponsors not only the Sunday morning church-at-home programs but the late-night "700 Club," a parallel to secular television's popular talk shows. There are also national service agencies such as the Evangelical Family Service, the Evangelical Child and Family Agency, Family Ministers, Evangelical Purchasing Service, and Universal Travel Services and commissions such as the Evangelism and Home Missions Association, Evangelical Social Action, Higher Education Stewardship, Women's Fellowship, and World Relief. Finally, in a miscellaneous category one could note the Christian Yellow Page Service, which lists Christian businesses nationally; the Christian Service Brigade, a type of Evangelical boy scouts; and the Christian Service Corps, the Evangelical equivalent of the Peace Corps. There are many other distinctly Evangelical parallel institutions, and all taken together compose vast social structure.

The Composite Profile

According to current survey research findings, contemporary American Evangelicalism is a predominantly white, disproportionally female religious

phenomenon. Its overall population is generally older than among other religious bodies. The clear majority of this population is married. Moreover,
the largest concentrations of American Evangelicalism are found in the rural,
small-town areas of the South and the west central and mid-Atlantic regions,
and in the medium-size cities of the South and Midwest. Evangelicals are
grossly under represented in the large cities. They are most greatly represented in the lower echelons of educational achievement, income level,
and occupational status; they fall mostly in the lower middle and working
classes. Evangelicals also surprisingly tend more to be Democratic than Republican or independent, though this does not hold constant when controlling for the various indexes of social class. Finally, they are firmly established in the denominational structure of American Protestantism.[2]

Apart from being an informative description, does this profile have any
bearing on the overall issue guiding this research, namely the relationship
between modernity and contemporary American Evangelicalism? Is it possible
to begin to locate Evangelicalism in relation to modernity? The answer is
yes, in limited ways. In the most general sense, one may locate Evangelicalism and other religious bodies in terms of their relative proximity to
modernity. In virtually all ways, Evangelicalism is located furthest from the
institutional structures and processes of modernity. In this regard, the secularists provide a helpful contrast at the other extreme, as a group perhaps
closest to those processes. In what specific dimensions, then, can one measure general proximity to modernity?

To begin, there is the gender composition of each group. Evangelicalism
finds its greatest popular support among women. A large percentage of
Evangelical men are older and retired. Thus a sizable proportion of Evangelicals are protected within the private sphere from the constraining forces
of the highly rational public sphere. In contrast, the secularists are mostly
young men in the professions and skilled-laborer and tradesmen occupations
and thus interact most frequently within the public sphere. Another dimension on which one can measure relative proximity to modernity is the geographic. As Baily (cited in Handy, 1971) noted in reference to late nineteenth-century and early twentieth-century America, "The rural hegemony
of the South was little disturbed by the immigration, industrialization, new
intellectual currents and all those other forces which were elsewhere trans-
forming society" (p. 69). The same could be said of the rural areas of the
Midwest and the mid-Atlantic region, and in the main it holds true today.
By virtue of their concentration in these areas, Evangelicals once again avoid
the constant and inevitable contact with the constraining forces of modernity. In contrast, the secularists are found most predominantly in the
intensely urban areas of the Northeast and the Rocky Mountain/Pacific regions. Finally, there are the various indexes of social class. Occupation has
already been mentioned in conjunction with age. Another index of social

class is education. Contemporary Evangelicals are among the poorest educated of religious groups. Thus they have not been exposed at length to the secularizing forces of public education—the veritable classroom for the inculcation of the world view of modernity. Secularists, on the other hand, are among those with the longest exposure to the modernizing influence of public educational institutions. Last, there is income. By virtue of being in the lower echelons of the distribution of income, Evangelicals are denied the social and geographic mobility available to those with greater incomes, and with it, first hand exposure to differing lifestyles and world views. At the opposite pole are the secularists, who, when age is considered, are high in income acquisition.

The collective interaction of these demographic factors clearly confirms the initial proposition that the Evangelical community as a whole is— perhaps more than any other major American religious body—sociologically and geographically distant from the institutional structures and processes of modernity. The demographic evidence also suggests that secularists and non-Christians are closest to those structures and processes. Liberal Protestants and Catholics could be similarly located in terms of their relative proximity to modernity.

In Chapter 2, I contended that the structural forces and symbols of modernity are inimical to the religious world view. If this is true, it is logical to hypothesize that the closer in proximity a person or group is to the functional rationality, the cultural pluralism, and the structural pluralism of modernity, the less likely it is that the person or group will be committed to religious belief and religious activism. Reciprocally, the further the proximity, the more likely the religious commitment. The combined demographic evidence supports these general hypotheses: that modernity does militate against the maintenance of traditional religious world views and that, as such, conservative or traditional religious meaning systems are most easily sustained the further away they are from modernity's structural and symbolic constraints. Thus one reason for the survival of American Evangelicalism in the modern world may be that its social and demographic distance from modernity allows it to avoid sustained confrontation with modernity's most threatening attributes.

Modernity is here to stay; its structures, processes, and symbols continue to be predominant in American society and culture. Although Evangelicalism is relatively distanced from it, that distance does not approach a total separation. There is a constant though not always intense interaction between the two phenomena, and the nature of that interaction is central to the problem at hand.

5

Beliefs and Practices

It is indisputable that contemporary Evangelicalism represents a distinctive conservative tradition within the religious history of the American people. As a theological tradition it has attempted to remain bonded to the legacy of apostolic and Reformational orthodoxy (variously understood). Elaborating the central doctrines of American Evangelicalism and other dimensions of the Evangelical world view and examining various Evangelical religious practices in relation to other religious traditions can help to clarify the phenomenon of Evangelicalism. These efforts can also provide a further basis for interpreting the social location of Evangelicalism relative to the structures and processes of modernity.

Evangelical Theology: The View of the Man on the Street

Perhaps the most important element of Evangelical theology is its particular conception of the Bible as the literary vehicle for God's revelation, both of his own nature and of his intentions in human history. As the inspired testimony of a perfect and supreme deity, the Bible is itself perfect, inerrant (which is to say, entirely without error of any kind), and infallible with regard to all spiritual, ethical, and religious matters.[1] It is, in the spirit of the Reformation, the final authority in matters that pertain to spiritual and everyday reality. The Bible, therefore, and not traditional prescriptions or ecclesiastical edicts, is to be trusted as the sole authoritative testimony to absolute truth.[2]

Corresponding to this conception of the biblical literature is a particular methodology for interpreting the Scriptures. As I have said, a commonsense literalism employing "lower criticism" has come to be regarded as the normative hermeneutic. The Bible is to be understood "in its plain and obvious sense." Concerning ethical, moral, and historical matters, the Bible is to be understood literally. Only in the poetic imagery (for example, in the Psalms,

61

Proverbs, Song of Solomon, and parts of the Revelation of St. John) is the metaphorical nature of the Bible acknowledged. No part of the Bible is ever regarded as mythical, folkloric, or imaginary.

A literalistic reading of the biblical literature provides the basis for the Evangelical metaphysic. The survey data reveals that this generally applies to the Evangelical population as a whole (see Table 5.1). While all Evangelicals believe in the inerrancy of Scripture, roughly two-thirds of all Evangelicals claim the Bible is the most important religious authority. This compares to much lower percentages among liberal Protestants, Catholics, non-Christians, and secularists.

In accordance with the Reformational world view and unlike many streams within liberal Christianity, Evangelicals interpret reality as both material and spiritual—as inhabited by both physical and spiritual beings. All of the essential features of Protestant orthodoxy are acknowledged and affirmed. In the spiritual realm there is an immutable, self-existent, omnipotent, omniscient, and omnipresent deity. The doctrine of the Trinity is very much affirmed: One Being with three personalities—Father, Son, and Holy Spirit. He is all goodness, all truth, all love, and all justice and righteousness. He is the creator of both the spiritual and the natural worlds. Part of the former are angels—spiritual beings enlisted in the service of God.

In opposition to God and his spiritual entourage is the personification of evil, Satan (the Devil, Lucifer, the Enemy, etc.) and his contingent of demonic forces. In Reformational theology, the Devil is regarded as a spiritual being and not merely a symbol of evil. Official contemporary Evangelical theology maintains this position, which is shared by contemporary Evangelical laity to a greater extent than in any other major religious group in America (see Table 5.2). Of all Evangelicals, two-thirds believe that the "Devil is a personal being who directs evil forces and influences people to do wrong," compared to much lower percentages among other groups. Of all Evangelicals, roughly 28 percent believe that the Devil is an "impersonal force" that influences people to do wrong, whereas only about 5 percent believe that the Devil does not exist either as a being or a force. In the spiritual realm, God and the Devil wage spiritual warfare against one another. It is a contest that has consequences for humankind in space and time.

In Reformational theology, it is also argued that God, who is life itself, created the earth and all life—vegetation and inhabitants. The origin of man began with God's creation of Adam and Eve after his own image. Among contemporary Evangelicals, this is still the predominant view (see Table 5.2). In the national sample, 81.6 percent of all Evangelicals held to this position. Most (13.2%) of the remaining Evangelicals believe that "God began an evolutionary cycle for all living things, including man, but personally intervened at a point in time and transformed man into a human being in his own image." Only 3.5 percent of all Evangelicals believe that

TABLE 5.1

SOURCE OF RELIGIOUS AUTHORITY BY RELIGIOUS PREFERENCE (in percentages)

	Evangelical	Liberal	Catholic	Non-Christian	Secularist
Church	3.5	5.4	29.4	3.8	0.0
Religious leaders	0.9	7.7	9.5	26.9	7.2
Holy Spirit	25.4	29.8	27.3	19.2	25.0
Bible	67.6	44.7	25.3	11.5	16.9
None	0.3	6.2	5.4	28.9	31.5
No opinion	2.3	6.2	3.1	9.7	19.4
	100.0	100.0	100.0	100.0	100.0
N =	(347)	(540)	(474)	(56)	(132)

TABLE 5.2

BELIEFS ABOUT THE DEVIL, ORIGIN OF MAN,
AND CONSOLATION FROM BELIEFS BY RELIGIOUS PREFERENCE (in percentages)

Views of the Devil	Evangelical	Liberal	Catholic	Non-Christian	Secularist
The Devil is a personal *being* who directs evil forces and influences people to do wrong.					
	66.8	26.7	32.6	6.3	17.1
The Devil is an impersonal *force* that influences people to do wrong.					
	28.4	46.0	46.7	25.0	27.3
The Devil does not exist, either as a being or a force.					
	4.8	27.3	20.7	68.7	55.6
	100.0	100.0	100.0	100.0	100.0

Views on the origin of man

God created Adam and Eve, which was the start of human life.					
	81.6	47.7	48.3	13.0	21.8
God began an evolutionary cycle for all living things, including man, but personally intervened at a point in time and transformed man into a human being in his own image.					
	13.2	25.5	27.2	10.9	14.5
God began an evolutionary cycle for all living things, including man, but *did not* personally intervene at a point in time and transform man into a human being in his own image.					
	3.5	14.1	13.0	41.3	13.6
The origin of man is unknown.					
	1.7	12.7	11.5	34.8	50.1
	100.0	100.0	100.0	100.0	100.0

Degree of consolation from beliefs

	Evangelical	Liberal	Catholic	Non-Christian	Secularist
A lot	82.1	45.6	55.1	18.2	23.0
Fair amount	17.0	38.2	36.0	34.1	37.8
Little	0.9	13.2	7.8	31.8	25.7
None	0.0	3.0	1.1	15.9	13.5
	100.0	100.0	100.0	100.0	100.0
N =	(347)	(540)	(474)	(56)	(132)

God began an evolutionary process but did not personally intervene to fashion man into his own image; only 1.7 percent of all Evangelicals believe that the origin of man is unknown.

Evangelicals also believe that man, out of his own free choice, rebelled against his creator. The result was a fall from God's special favor and thus a condemnation to an eternal separation from God. In the temporal world, this meant that human experience would be characterized by suffering, pain, anguish and grief. In the after life, it meant man would experience the eternal torment of the fires of hell. Yet God provided a means by which man could escape this punishment. The fulfillment of God's promise of salvation began with the performance of certain sacrificial rites and the faithful obedience to the Law of Moses and culminated with the advent of the promised Jewish Messiah, Jesus Christ. By personally intervening in human history, in the historic person of Jesus (the incarnation), God provided, once and for all, the means by which all mankind could find eternal salvation from damnation. Christ's perfect life, sacrificial death, and bodily resurrection from the dead opened the way for all to be restored to favor with God. History, from the time of Christ to the day of judgment, would be the history of God's people announcing the fulfillment of the divine plan of redemption to "all peoples of all nations" so that "all might hear and believe."

In this context it is appropriate to examine contemporary Evangelical soteriology. Salvation for the individual, as conceived in this world view, is based on the belief that God, in Christ, personally died for our sins and thus forgives us all our sins. Yet it becomes clear on closer scrutiny that belief is not sufficient in itself, as can be seen from this account of an encounter Bill Bright, president of the Campus Crusade for Christ, had with a woman:

> At the conclusion of my talk this young woman said to me, "I don't think that I am a Christian, and I have always had doubts about my salvation. Through the years, I have gone to different ministers, and to other Christian leaders for spiritual counsel. I have told them I was not sure that I was a Christian. They have inevitably responded, 'Well, you believe that Jesus is the Son of God, don't you? You believe that Christ died on the cross for your sins, don't you?' 'Yes,' I would answer. 'Well, then you are a Christian. Don't worry about it. Let's pray, and you just believe that you are a Christian.' But I have never been sure that God heard my prayer. There has been no evidence that Christ has come in. I am afraid that I will die without Christ." That day I had the privilege of sharing the good news with this dear young woman who had been exposed to Christianity throughout her entire life. This time the Holy Spirit enabled her to trust God and His Word. By faith she received the Lord Jesus, the gracious gift of God's love. Her heart was filled with joy and praise. (Bright, 1971:no 6, pp. 15–16)

More than believing, there is an additional (though tacit) requirement that one must be "born again" by receiving Jesus Christ as one's personal

Lord and Savior. This is accomplished by asking Jesus Christ to come into one's life. By doing so, one establishes a "personal relationship with God," and "Christianity is at heart a personal relationship with God" (Richards, 1977:11). There is some diversity within Evangelicalism as to the necessity of being born again, diversity that often follows denominational lines (e.g., the Anabaptist and Reformational-Confessional traditions typically emphasize the confessional as opposed to the conversional basis of salvation). Owing to the predominance of the Baptist tradition in mainstream Evangelicalism, the soteriological emphasis within Evangelicalism is on a specific turning point in a person's biography. Among contemporary American Evangelicals interviewed, 94.2 percent reported having had a conversion experience at an identifiable point that included asking Jesus Christ to be their Lord and Savior (see Appendix 1). In many circles, knowledge of the specific time, day, and place in which this experience occurs is accorded pre-eminence, as though such knowledge was itself a central aspect of the salvation process.

Everyday life as an Evangelical involves continued personal communion with God and reliance on the imminent strength and wisdom of God present through the Holy Spirit to meet the demands and pressures of life in an alien (i.e., sinful) world. The Evangelical's life is frequently likened to a "walk with God." The consequences of this communion are important for gauging the efficacy of the Evangelical theodicy (see Table 5.2). According to the survey data, roughly 82 percent of all Evangelicals claim to receive "a lot of consolation from their beliefs about God." This compares with 55.1 percent of Catholics, 45.6 percent of liberal Protestants, 23.0 percent of secularists, and 18.2 percent of non-Christians.

The Religious Practices of Evangelicals

It is apparent that Evangelicals, as a population, do retain a proportionately higher degree of adherence to the traditionally defined components of the Judeo-Christian heritage than other religious groups in this tradition. They also receive a proportionately higher degree of consolation from their particular beliefs. This was in many ways predictable, as it is predictable that Evangelicals will be more assiduous in following traditional religious practices. The data generally confirm this.

On Bible reading, Evangelicals clearly rank higher than do all others (see Table 5.3). Of all Evangelicals 35.5 percent surveyed read the Bible once a day or more; 35.8 percent read between one and three times a week; 10.1 percent read one to three times per month; and 18.6 percent either read the Bible less than once per month or not at all. Liberal Protestants follow far behind at 8.5, 17.6, 14.5, and 59.4 percent respectively. Catholics, non-Christians, and secularists follow in declining order, with even lower frequencies of Bible reading. Whereas the pattern generally holds among Evangelicals when controlling for such variables as income, education, age, and race, there is a notable difference when controlling for work status (Gallup, 1980a). As one might predict, those Evangelicals who are employed in the work force full time generally read the Bible less than those who do not work at all.

As shown in Chapter 4, a greater percentage of Evangelicals are church (broadly defined to include synagogues, etc.) members than those of any other religious preference (see Table 4.6). Of those belonging to a church, Evangelicals, as a population, claim to be more meaningfully involved in their church than are members of any other group (see Table 5.4). This claim is buttressed by the fact that nearly twice as many Evangelicals perform volunteer work for their church as do liberal Protestants, Catholics, and non-Christians (see Table 5.4).

As one might predict from this involvement, Evangelicals far surpass all other religious groups in church or religious service attendance (see Table 5.4), with 62.2 percent of all Evangelicals attending once a week or more, 15.4 percent attending one to three times a month, and 22.4 percent either attending less than once per month or not attending at all. Catholics follow with 45.3 percent attending once per week or more, 16.5 percent one to three times a month, and 38.2 percent attending less than once per month or not at all. Liberal Protestants, non-Christians, and secularists follow successively, with significantly lower frequencies of church or religious service attendance. Among Evangelicals, the pattern remains basically the same when controlling for income, race, and gender. When controlling for work status, once again, those who work part time or who do not work at all show a greater frequency of church attendance than do those who work full time (Gallup, 1980a).

Meaningful commitment to a religious belief system may also be marked by the financial commitment a person makes to his church or other religious organization; and in tithing, American Evangelicals again stand far above all other religious groups (see Table 5.4). Of those sampled, 44.4 percent of all Evangelicals claimed to give 10 percent or more of their income to their church or to another religious organization; 17.8 percent gave 5 to 9 percent of their income; 25.7 percent gave less than 5 percent; and 12.1 percent did not contribute any portion of their income. This compares with a breakdown of liberal Protestants, 13.5 percent of whom claimed to tithe 10 percent or more of their income, 15.6 percent of whom claimed to tithe 5 to 9 percent, 37.6 percent of whom gave less than 5 percent, and one-third of whom did not give anything at all. Catholics and non-Christians follow, closely paralleling each other at the higher levels of giving, varying at the lower levels.

A final behavioral dimension of religiosity is the degree to which people share their religious beliefs with others not of their faith in the attempt to

TABLE 5.3

BIBLE READING BY RELIGIOUS PREFERENCE (in percentages)

	Evangelical	Liberal	Catholic	Non-Christian	Secularist
Daily or more	35.5	8.5	4.3	6.1	1.7
1–3 times a week	35.8	17.6	10.7	8.2	4.2
1–3 times a month	10.1	14.5	12.5	8.2	6.8
Less than monthly	18.6	59.4	72.5	77.5	87.3
	100.0	100.0	100.0	100.0	100.0
N =	(347)	(540)	(474)	(56)	(132)

TABLE 5.4

CHURCH PARTICIPATION BY RELIGIOUS PREFERENCE (in percentages)

	Evangelical	Liberal	Catholic	Non-Christian	Secularist
Meaningful involvement in church					
Yes	93.5	84.1	81.3	84.0	71.4
No	6.5	15.9	18.7	16.0	28.6
	100.0	100.0	100.0	100.0	100.0
Volunteer work in religious organization					
Yes	64.2	36.0	37.7	38.0	5.5
No	35.8	64.0	62.3	62.0	94.5
	100.0	100.0	100.0	100.0	100.0
Church attendance					
Weekly or more	62.2	23.1	45.3	13.2	2.5
1–3 times a month	15.4	18.7	16.5	11.3	5.0
Less than monthly	22.4	58.2	38.2	75.5	92.5
	100.0	100.0	100.0	100.0	100.0
Tithing					
10%	44.4	13.5	7.7	6.1	1.6
5–9%	17.8	15.6	17.0	14.3	1.6
Less than 5%	25.7	37.6	52.2	40.8	16.4
None	12.1	33.3	23.1	38.8	80.4
	100.0	100.0	100.0	100.0	100.0
N =	(347)	(540)	(474)	(56)	(132)

proselytize. Clearly, in the Evangelical subculture, evangelism is considered the first priority, with the spiritual well-being of one's family and oneself being second (see Table 5.5). Among all other religious groups, spiritual well-being was considered to be the highest priority for Christians. This attitude is reflected in the amount Evangelicals proselytize as compared to the other religious groups: 15 percent of all Evangelicals, at least once a

TABLE 5.5

CHRISTIAN PRIORITIES AND EVANGELISM BY RELIGIOUS PREFERENCE (in percentages)

Christian priorities	Evangelical	Liberal	Catholic	Non-Christian	Secularist
Evangelism	51.3	23.1	16.2	4.3	10.0
Spiritual growth	29.3	42.7	47.7	53.2	35.5
Community involvement	6.5	19.2	17.3	31.9	37.3
Local church	11.1	8.6	11.0	4.3	2.7
Political involvement	1.8	6.4	7.8	6.3	14.5
	100.0	100.0	100.0	100.0	100.0
Evangelism					
Daily	15.0	7.8	6.8	7.8	6.6
Once a week	22.8	9.8	11.3	15.7	6.7
Once a month	15.3	12.5	15.5	11.8	10.0
Less than monthly	24.1	28.7	26.9	31.4	21.7
Never	22.8	41.2	39.5	33.3	55.0
	100.0	100.0	100.0	100.0	100.0
N =	(347)	(540)	(474)	(56)	(132)

day; 22.8 percent, at least once per week; 15.3 percent, at least once per month; 24.1 percent, less than once every month; and 22.8 percent, not at all. Liberal Protestants, Catholics, and non-Christians closely parallel each other along this dimension, with frequencies much lower than those within Evangelicalism. Secularists, as expected, share whatever religious beliefs they have less than all others. Of all those with no religious preference, 55 percent claim never to share their beliefs at all.

Conclusions

The survey data generally confirm what is typically thought to be true about American Evangelicalism relative to other groups. Evangelicals, on the whole, remain embedded in a world view in which the perceived spiritual or supernatural dimensions of reality play intimately and intricately in everyday life. At the cognitive level, their foundation is the Bible as the inspired and therefore inerrant Word of God and the final authority by which one may test the verity of religious beliefs. While all Evangelicals believe in addition in the humanity and divinity of the historical Christ, as well as in the efficacy of the salvific act of Christ's life, death, and resurrection, the majority of Evangelicals also continue to believe that the Devil, as the personification of evil, is a power to be contended with in everyday life. It is frequently claimed that "Satan and demonic forces continue to the present to lie to and deceive the followers of Jesus Christ as well as those who are outside of God's grace." Moreover, a majority of Evangelicals hold the biblicist belief that the origin of man began with God's creation of Adam and Eve. Although the clear majority maintain these biblicist beliefs, the diversity of opinion among Evangelicals on the last two central doctrines is noteworthy. It is suggestive of the beginnings of an erosion of confidence in the legitimacy of traditional theistic interpretations of human history.

Notwithstanding the lack of unanimity, this overall supernaturalistic orientation both is encouraged by and encourages a number of religious practices. Bible reading is significantly higher among Evangelicals than among other groups in the Christian tradition. Meaningful involvement in a church or other religious organization is also much greater among Evangelicals than other religious bodies. This is measured by a number of indexes: church membership, church or religious service attendance, performing volunteer work for a church organization, and financial commitment to a church, parachurch, or another religious organization. Along all of these indexes, Evangelicals predictably rank higher than all other religious groups. Finally, Evangelicals exhibit a much greater commitment to lay proselytization. It is evident that traditional expressions of faith are more operative in the everyday lives of Evangelicals than they are in the lives of those of other religious persuasions. The ostensible result is that Evangelicals can claim to derive a greater personal consolation from their religious belief system than do those in other religious groups.

In the interpretive framework of this analysis, the anachronistic character of the contemporary Evangelical world view relative to other religious world views may be accounted for by the fact of Evangelicals' greater demographic distance from the institutional structures and processes of modernity than any other religious group. The contact between this world view and the world-disaffirming structures and processes of modernity is less intense, and therefore the latter is less threatening. Conversely, such a distance affords a more agreeable situation in which to maintain the world view of conservative Protestantism as cognitively plausible and behaviorally viable. This conclusion is buttressed by the fact that frequencies of two of the most important measures of religious commitment—Bible reading and church attendance—shift when controlling for work status. The frequencies are lower for those who have greater everyday exposure to the public sphere. Although this may also be a function of full-time work leaving less time for these activities, it is fair to assume that exposure to a functionally rational public sphere does have a negative effect on these dimensions of religiosity.

Part Three

THE DYNAMICS OF COGNITIVE BARGAINING

6

Accommodation: The Domestication of Belief

As a result of its varied encounter with modernity in the past century, Evangelicalism has slowly undergone a variety of subtle changes, the general direction and contour of which I have sketched. Of specific importance at this juncture is the issue of accommodation. Through the interchange that necessarily occurs between the social structure and the culture, does this form of religious orthodoxy, in spite of its intransigence, yield notable concessions to the more dominant structural and symbolic forces of modernity? If so, in what ways does adjustment take place? I pursue the answers to these questions in the context of the three structural dimensions of modernity discussed in Chapter 2: rationality, cultural pluralism, and structural pluralism. Along each of these dimensions a measure of accommodation is predictable; the character and degree of accommodation is the central question.

Rationalization and the Codification
of Evangelical Spirituality

As perhaps the dominant structural characteristic of modernity, rationality imposes constraints on the culture and therefore on the world views of individuals in modern societies—constraints that make accommodation almost impossible to resist. The Protestant experience does not present fundamental opposition to such constraints. The cognitive styles of the Protestant world view and the modern world view have certain similarities that are historically grounded and dialectically related. One may note the Weberian commonplace that the innerworldly asceticism of early Protestantism was particularly suited for the augmentation of rationality in Western society. Even as Western rationality and techniques began to develop independently of religion, the world view of Protestantism continued to legitimate modern rationality and even to reflect some of its changes. Clearly, there is a historical carry-over; the affinities remain constant to the present. This is so with regard to contemporary Evangelicalism, yet there appear to be noteworthy differences between the rationalism expressed in early Protestantism and that found in contemporary Evangelicalism.

For the Puritan, the rationalism that inhered in his world view (expressed most profoundly as discipline, perseverence, thrift, etc.) was particularly oriented toward the behavioral and ethical dimensions of his experience, especially as it pertained to vocation, education, and other aspects of public life (Greven, 1977). It was also clearly evidenced in the behavioral and ethical dimensions of the more private matters of child rearing, marriage, and worship. Dimensions of this ethical rationalism continue to provide dominant themes in contemporary Evangelicalism, and in this sense the world view of present-day Evangelicalism is entirely compatible with modernity.

The cognitive aspects of the Puritan world view were not, however, so intensely rationalized. A simple, almost irrational quality pervaded Puritan understanding of the more mundane activities of everyday life, the spiritual, and the sublime. The promulgation of this understanding in the community and the socialization of children into Christian living occurred principally through precedent and example rather than rational edicts (Morgan, 1966). Reality, especially spiritual reality, was simply understood, propositionally self-evident. Modernity brings about not only the rationalization of behavior but of consciousness as well. Whereas Protestantism has always been compatible with modern rationalism at the behavioral level, its most conservative factions have found an alliance with modern rationalism at the cognitive level to be an uneasy one. Conservative Protestantism as a whole has been slow, even reluctant, to accommodate to the pressure to rationalize its world view. The recognition of this reluctance has prompted the popular accusation of anti-intellectualism.

The constraint to accommodate appears to have been too great to resist entirely. The first significant movement to rationalize the world view of Evangelicalism occurred after the founding of the NAE, among its spokesmen, in their attempt to provide conservative Protestantism with a plausible apologetic. Only later did accommodation occur as a wider scale subcultural phenomenon. In the process, it assumed a particular form: the increasing methodization and standardization of spirituality.

This is not to say that this is a new phenomenon. To be sure, eighteenth- and nineteenth-century Protestantism did reveal clear propensities for the rationalization of spirituality. The rise of Methodism is a good example. What is different about contemporary American Evangelicalism is the intensification of this propensity to unprecedented proportions. This intensification comes about as an adaptation to modern rationality. Thus one may note the increasing tendency to translate the specifically religious components of the Evangelical world view, previously understood to be plain, self-evident, and without need of elaboration, into rigorously standardized prescriptions. The spiritual aspects of Evangelical life are increasingly approached by means of and interpreted in terms of "principals," "rules," "steps," "laws," "codes," "guidelines," and such. The proliferation in the Evangelical book market of how-to manuals for channeling the many dimensions of Christian life is evidence of this tendency. Bright has offered this justification:

> God's Plan was our first written "how to" material—that is, material which explains simply and specifically how an individual can arrive at a desired goal, and also how he, in turn, can help others to arrive at the same goal. The "how to" approach is one of the most needed and most powerful approaches to the Christian life and witness I know anything about. (Bright, 1971:no. 6, p. 18)

From the very start of a person's career as an Evangelical, he is immersed in a world view that is highly formulated and systematized. Even the means by which a person becomes an Evangelical are highly methodized. Although Billy Graham in *How To Be Born Again* (1977) qualified his presentation by claiming there is no single "tidy little formula" for receiving salvation, he quickly offered "some guidelines from the Bible which will help you accept Jesus Christ as your Lord and Savior"—guidelines labeled by his evangelistic organization as "Four Steps to Peace with God":

> First, you must recognize what God did: that He loved you so much He gave His Son to die on the cross. Second, you must repent for your sins. It's not enough to be sorry; repentance is that turnabout from sin that is emphasized. Third, you must receive Jesus Christ as Savior and Lord. This means that you cease trying to save yourself and accept Christ without reservation. Fourth, you must confess Christ publicly. This confession is a sign that you have been converted. (Graham, 1977.167–168)

Graham's presentation is typical of what one finds in mainstream American Evangelicalism. An approximation of this methodization holds constant in the subculture regardless of social diversity. Inter-Varsity Christian Fellowship literature as well as "The Old Time Gospel Hour" broadcast employ similar prescriptions.

Other versions of this phenomenon are readily available in Evangelical literature and readily apparent in Evangelical circles. One is worth mentioning as perhaps the most unusual example of the methodization of the conversion process; it is found in the widely known and widely distributed (100 million copies) pamphlet entitled *The Four Spiritual Laws* (1965), written by Bright. The tract might be best described as an exercise in spiritual positivism. Bright begins by claiming that "just as there are physical laws that govern the physical universe, so are there spiritual laws which govern your relationship with God." Conversion transpires through acknowledging the validity of each of the four laws and by following the specific instructions on how one "receives Jesus Christ as Savior and Lord."

> Law One. God loves you, and offers a wonderful plan for your life. Law Two. Man is sinful and separated from God. Therefore, he cannot know and experience God's love and plan for his life. Law Three. Jesus Christ is God's only provision for man's sin. Through him you can know and experience God's love and plan for your life. Law Four. We must individually receive Jesus Christ as Savior and Lord; then we can know and experience God's love and plan for our lives. . . . Receiving Christ involves turning to God from self (repentance) and trusting Christ to come into our lives to forgive our sins and to make us the kind of people He wants us to be. (Bright, 1965)

With both Bright and Graham, the presentation is followed by a suggested prayer formulated with all of the ingredients necessary for being born again:

> Lord Jesus, I need You. Thank You for dying on the cross for my sins. I open the door of my life and receive You as my Savior and Lord. Thank You for forgiving my sins and giving me eternal life. Take control of the throne of my life. Make me the kind of person You want me to be. (Graham, 1977)

The systematization of the gospel to its "distilled essence," as Bright has labeled it, and the methodization of the conversion process into a series of procedures makes a convenient package for the potential convert to appropriate. This appropriation is only the requisite first step to becoming an Evangelical; many more packages are designed to guide a person in all dimensions of his spiritual career. A spiritual positivism is all-pervading.

Because a literal reading of the Biblical literature provides the metaphysical foundation for the Evangelical world view, a firm biblicism constitutes a notable feature of the Evangelical's cognitive style. While biblicism has remained constant in conservative Protestantism, the linguistic style in which it has been couched by contemporary Evangelicals has become modified to sound more empirical. Stanford (1976) demonstrated this trend clearly when he wrote:

> And this is all important, true faith must be based solely upon scriptural facts. . . . Unless our faith is established on facts, it is no more than conjecture, superstition, speculation or presumption. Once we begin to reckon (count) on facts, our Father begins to build us up in the faith. (p. 7)

In the same chapter Stanford quoted Alexander R. Hay—"Faith must be based on certainty. There must be definite knowledge of God's purpose and will. Without that there can be no true faith. Faith needs facts to rest upon"—and Evan Hopkins—"God in His Word reveals to us the facts with which faith has to deal" (p. 9). In much of the literature published by

Campus Crusade for Christ, this same theme is stressed. Fact (God and his Word) provides the basis for faith (trust in God and his Word) and all other subsequent spiritual growth. Granting that spiritual reality may be as "real" as physical or natural reality, describing the reality to which scripture speaks in the same manner in which the natural scientist might describe biologic constants, for example, does not amply account for the qualitative differences between the two phenomena. Yet the ontological equality of physical and spiritual reality is forcefully implied by the couching of theology in the grammar of empiricism. Inasmuch as this linguistic style pervades the interpretation of biblical literature, it follows that it will carry over into all other dimensions of Evangelical spirituality and spiritual growth. A review of popular Evangelical literature bears this out.

It is nearly universally agreed within Evangelicalism that there are at least three activities essential for spiritual growth: Bible reading, prayer, and giving public testimony to one's faith. In what ways have Evangelicals accommodated each of these areas to the pragmatic rationality of modernity? The first ingredient is a regular reading of God's Word. "It [the Bible] is God's instrument of salvation . . . and God's instrument for growing mature Christians. It is the blueprint for the Christian" (Sweeting, 1976a:59). Indeed, a disciplined reading of the Bible provides a subjective measure of verification that one is saved for, we are told, "God has put His holy hunger for the Word in your heart" (Cook, 1978a:66).

Beyond mere prescriptions to faithfully attend to Bible reading, the popular literature on the dynamics of spiritual growth delineates guidelines for maximizing the benefits of time spent in this manner. In these guidelines there is a measure of variability, however. Graham (1977), for example, encourages his readers to first "pray before you read" and second, "memorize portions of the Word of God" (p. 180). Richards (1977) suggests a "simple 'step by step' approach":

a. Read the Bible daily, asking God to show what you need to understand that day.
b. When God does show you something, act on what He says.
c. If you feel hesitant or afraid, remember how much God loves you, and He wants you to know the very best. Trust the Holy Spirit, your Helper, to give you the strength to obey. (p. 76)

Sweeting (1976a) has provided a further elaboration of such guidelines: "To grow in the things of God, we should read the Bible prayerfully" (to gain the "illumination of the Holy Spirit"), "carefully" ("requiring concentration"), "systematically" ("at a prescribed time, in a quiet place . . . begin at the beginning, . . . learn the facts, then apply them"), and "trustfully" (because without faith, it is impossible to please God) (pp. 59–66). In still another manual, specific instructions are presented:

Take your Bible and open it to the book through which you happen to be reading. Get on your knees, and ask God in Jesus' name to speak to you from His Word. Read, and reread the passage until, in the stillness of your heart, God, the Holy Spirit says something . . . from the Word . . . just for you! When He does, get paper and a pen and write it down. Now, still on your knees before God, pray back to Him what He said to your heart. Pray, on the basis of God's Word to you, until your very soul is aflame with the message. Then arise and proceed to put into action that which God has put into your life. Share with someone as soon as possible the blessings you received through eating the Word. (Cook, 1978a:69)

Within this general format are a nearly infinite number of specific methods of studying the Bible. All of these provide evidence of the methodization of this area of spiritual concern.

A second ingredient considered essential for spiritual development is prayer. Prayer is defined in the popular imagination as "simply communicating with God," or "talking to God and having Him talk to us." It is often likened to a "hotline of direct communication with God, available to [the Christian] at all times," or the "conversation that would take place between friends" (Bright, 1971:no. 6, p. 9 f.). In addition, it is described as involving "crying out to God," "calling upon God at every occasion of need in your life," and "confession and cleansing" (Swecting, 1976a:69). Formal prayer, because it is presumably less personal and less spontaneous, is deemed less real and less valuable in the eye of God: "Let us have done with cold, formal, heartless praying. It grieves the heart of God and leaves our own lives more poverty stricken than they were before" (Cook, 1978a:82).

In this area of spirituality as well, much more is offered than general prescriptions to "diligently and without ceasing, seek the Lord in prayer and in meditation upon His Word." There is a slight contradiction here. While prayer is to be personal and spontaneous (and not formal), guidelines as well as specific methods of praying are available to the Evangelical to assist him in these matters. One of the more popular guidelines is the ACTS formula (from Bright, 1971:no. 6). It is proposed that "certain basic elements should be included in prayer": adoration ("to worship and praise Him"), confession (of "our sin and worthlessness"), thanksgiving ("for all things"), and supplication ("intercession for others and petition for our own needs"). Though "not a rigid sequence," this formula does provide an informal inventory system for regulating one's prayer life, thus seeming to undermine the spontaneity and informality considered appropriate for prayer.

Just as in Puritan times, prayer for the Evangelical is supposed to be a continuous excercise throughout daily life, "any time, any where." The focus of teaching and encouragement has, however, become a relatively modern invention called the "quiet time" or "personal devotions," now viewed as "an indispensable ingredient for a successful Christian life" (Sweeting, 1976a:80). A qualification is necessary, however. Spending a disciplined period of time in prayer and meditation is not unique to the present age. Sixteenth-century Reformationists and later German Pietists, and English and New England Puritans as well were known to cultivate regular time for prayer; what is unique to the present is the increasing systematization and programming. This "quiet time" has been variously defined as "a time, generally at the beginning of the day, where you look into the Word of God and let God speak to you and when you pray and open your heart and in the process, of course, open up the whole day to God" (Cook, 1978b:230). One manual (Sweeting, 1976a:89) calls for "a definite time and place" each day; a suggested program follows:

> I would suggest that the quiet time begin with prayer to God, asking for His blessing on your time together. . . . Prayer time should include praise and thanksgiving for all God is doing and will do. Pray for your loved ones. Pray for others. Pray for yourself. After prayer, you'll want to read God's Word, His special message to you. . . . To meditate is to think quietly and deeply about the greatness and goodness of God. Notice the promises of God. Look for guiding principles for your daily life. Commit to memory a meaningful verse. Don't hurry. Regularly, quietly, systematically, yet leisurely, meditate upon the written Word and the living Word.

Representative of this tendency taken to unusual proportions is a document published by the Evangelical campus organization, the Navigators. Entitled *Seven Minutes with God* (R. Foster, n.d.), the tract justifies the need for a "workable plan on how to begin and maintain a Morning Watch" on the basis that it helps to create a "fixed and established heart" necessary to produce "stability in life." The author claims that the suggested program is "not a fetish but a guide." "Do not become devoted to a habit but to the Savior," says the author, although the proposal of such a program suggests otherwise. The author begins by exhorting his readers to "make an appointment with God" for seven minutes, seven days a week. After a brief overview, he summarizes as follows:

> Lets put these seven minutes together:
> 1/2 Prayer for guidance, Psalm 143:8
> 4   Reading the Bible, Psalm 119:18
> 2 1/2 Prayer: Adoration, I Chronicles 29:11 Confession, I John 1:9
> _____   Thanksgiving, Ephesians 5:20 Supplication, Matthew 7:7
> 7 minutes

Though it is clear that this pattern is not representative of the daily experience of all Evangelicals (indeed it is safe to assume that many Evangelicals do not schedule a quiet time at all), such instruction is an indication that the tendency to program is deemed appropriate and even desirable in mainstream American Evangelicalism.

The third activity requisite to spiritual growth is witnessing for Christ. Historically, the responsibility for Christian evangelization rested principally with a trained clerisy, and this was true even of the Protestant traditions that emphasized the spiritual significance of the laity. In the contemporary Evangelical subculture, however, the focus of responsibility is in fact on the laity. Touted as a privilege and a means of spiritual growth, it is clear that witnessing for Christ also provides a public index of a person's spiritual status. This focus, unique to Evangelicalism among traditional religions in America, is of course reflected in the high frequency of Evangelicals sharing their beliefs with those of a different religious persuasion.

As to the means of evangelization, it is clear that merely sharing one's faith with a non-Evangelical is not enough. This requirement, too, has become subject to rigorous systematization and methodization. Going beyond the exhortation to "go into all the world, telling the good news of Jesus Christ" are numerous programs available to Evangelicals detailing, with unusual complexity, strategies for effective evangelization. After all, it is reasoned, the "'know how' makes the difference between effective and ineffective witnessing" (Bright, 1971:no. 6, p. 13). Here again there is some variation of technique and degree of rationalization.

Exemplifying one of the more general strategies is a program offered by Cook (1978a); his "pointers for successful witnessing" are:

1. Get over the mental hurdle involved in "talking religion" to people.
2. Fill your mind and heart with the Word of God.
3. Begin each day with prayer for God's guidance and form the habit of watching throughout the day for the people God will send to you for your ministry to them.
4. Always rely on the Holy Spirit to tell you what to say.
5. Always press gently for some action NOW.
6. Follow through. (pp. 98, 99)

Campus Crusade for Christ, another example, vigorously defends the efficacy of the Four Spiritual Laws (Bright, 1965) as a technique for successful evangelization. They offer training programs in the use of the principles outlined in the pamphlet, and the technique remains one of the more popular strategies of student evangelization on the American scene.

Two more training programs deserve mentioning. One is summarized in a manual entitled *Training for Evangelism* (Sisson, 1979); the other is entitled *Evangelism Explosion* (Kennedy, 1977). Both manuals represent Promethean efforts in the rationalization of evangelistic techniques. The latter is particularly important not only for its widespread popularity in the Evangelical subculture but for the strong endorsement it receives from Billy Graham. Echoing the comment of another pastor, Graham has written: "[This program] is the most revolutionary technique for personal evangelism to mobilize the sleeping giant of our laity to be discovered in the twentieth century" (Kennedy, 1977:vii). A cursory review of this program is instructive.

The author begins by claiming that "the principles contained in the program represent some of the basic principles of the New Testament concerning the matter of [personal lay] evangelism" (Kennedy, 1977:1). What follows is similar to an elaborate market analysis. The major difference is not in the methods of marketing proposed but in the commodity being marketed. The two major markets to which the gospel is to be presented are those who are "church oriented" and those who are not: the "secular minded." Diagnostic questions are offered to determine a person's spiritual condition.

> Every science has progressed to the degree that its instruments of measurement have been developed. This is true in medicine. The foundation of good medicine is sound diagnosis. Where remedies are applied without such diagnosis we say that the practitioner is a "quack." This same truth applies to the spiritual realm. Unless we can accurately diagnose the person's spiritual condition we shall very likely endeavor to apply the wrong spiritual cure, or apply the right cure in the wrong manner. (Kennedy, 1977:52)

Different strategies then are proposed to account for the differences in orientation. Essential to success in both markets is an "understanding of the laws of persuasion or salesmanship." According to the author, "there are five great laws of selling or persuading: attention, interest, desire, conviction, and close. It does not matter whether you are selling a refrigerator or persuading men to accept a new idea or philosophy, the same basic laws of persuasion hold true" (Kennedy, 1977:46).

From this point, the program consists of an elaborately detailed guide for presentation and subsequent analysis of the Evangelical message. Included are the "proper use of the testimony" as a technique for proselytizing, "attitudes" and "specific methods for handling objections," a catalog of verbal illustrations for the elucidation of biblical principles, a list of the do's and don'ts of lay witnessing, specific procedures for following up the initial contact, and a systematically organized schedule for discipling the new believer. There are similarly constructed schedules for those who have made no profession of faith as well as for those who are Christians but are not active in a local church. From this beginning, varying levels of leadership within the local church are developed.

The chain of command consists of the following links:
1. Prayer partners
2. Trainees
3. Junior Trainers
4. Lieutenants
5. Assistant Lay Teachers/Trainers
6. Teachers/Trainers (lay and staff)

7. Leadership Clinic Administrators
8. Leadership Clinic Teachers. (Kennedy, 1977:223)

The ultimate goal for a person embarked on this program is to be certified as a lay clinic leader: "Certification gives uniform minimum standards of excellence with maximum potential for communication and multiplication. We feel it is an essential element in strategy for effective evangelization of the world" (Kennedy, 1977:15). In this way the rationalization process is completed.

In each of the three requisite areas of spirituality, a pragmatic rationalism is evident; it is equally evident in life planning. The deinstitutionalization of vocation and family social status, and therefore of traditional sources of personal identity, is tacitly acknowledged in the commonplace assumption that each Christian must endeavor to find "God's will for his life." God's will for such long-range considerations is not quite as apparent as it may have seemed in the past. In pursuing this objective, the Evangelical is aided by a number of readily available formulas. Here again, there is wide diversity. One such formula for testing a plan of action is contained in the metaphor of three harbor lights. If the biblical teaching, the subjective witness of the Holy Spirit, and one's life plan line up like harbor lights or are consonant with one another, it must be God's will and therefore one should proceed with the plan. Another method deserving particular mention is a ten-step formula for knowing God's will:

1. Be obedient to His already revealed will.
2. Be open to any means or results.
3. God's Word as the cornerstone to guidance.
4. A life of prayer.
5. The witness of the Holy Spirit.
6. The good council of other Christians.
7. Providential circumstances.
8. Careful evaluation of the foregoing.
9. The decision: to act or to wait.
10. The stamp of approval—God's peace. (Carlson, 1976:153, 156)

By following this formula, the author claims that one can "determine God's will for you in all of life's major decisions" from "planning your education" to "changing jobs" to "choosing a life mate" and so on. In this area of Christian life as well, the significant reduction of spirituality to rational formulas or a program is patent.

Although accommodation to modern rationality takes place primarily through codification or programming of the behavioral dimensions of spirituality, spirituality as a quality of the personality is also rationalized in many ways. The common phrases "taking one's spiritual temperature" and the "barometers of our spiritual maturity" suggest that spirituality can be measured. Based on this conception is the widely held notion that there are three human types: (1) "natural man" who "is not a Christian," whose "interests and ambitions are centered in things fleshly and worldly"; (2) "carnal man," a Christian who "desires and sometimes attempts to set his affections on the things of God but still holds on to the things of this world"; and (3) "spiritual man," "a Christian who is controlled and empowered by the Holy Spirit of God, . . . and his interests and ambitions . . . centered around and subject to the perfect will of God" (Bright, 1971:no. 2, p. 14).[1] The last two types are particularly germane to the issue at hand. The behavioral dimensions of spirituality (e.g., the amount of time a person spends reading the Bible, praying, tithing, witnessing, and orienting his life goals around God's will) all provide empirical indexes by which the differences between the carnal Christian and the spiritual Christian are elucidated in the Evangelical world view.

Thus, the rationality of modernity has clearly had a pronounced influence on the world view of American Evangelicalism. Yet the influence has been limited, for although it has entailed a rationalization of spirituality, it has not entailed the reduction of the supernatural elements of the world view to natural categories.

As Evangelicalism is not monolithic either in its structural characteristics or its cultural expression, so too its accommodation to the rationality of modernity is not uniform. Plainly, there is diversity. In charismatic circles, for instance, spirituality, though rationalized in ways similar to those I have outlined here, often also includes unroutinized charismatic excitement expressed through such phenomena as glossolalia, trance behavior, being "slain in the spirit," and the like.[2] But even in these instances, bursts of charismatic fervor typically take place in contexts where such behavior is highly institutionalized and expected. Exceptions notwithstanding, the dominant impulse in Evangelical spirituality is the increased tendency toward systematization, codification, and methodization. Among other things, this tendency allows for the packaging of spirituality—a phenomenon with far-reaching implications. At one level, the packaging of Evangelical faith is an example of what has been called the "primitivization of reality" (Zijderveld, 1970:80). This is a reduction of perceptions of reality to simplifications as a way of coping with the abstraction of modern experience. At another level, this packaging performs a more pragmatic function, as the example of the conversion process suggests.

Packaging the conversion process in a systematized fashion produces effects with parallels in market economics. In the rationalized economy, mass production allows for widespread distribution and consumption while maintaining a high degree of quality control over the product. Likewise the reduction of the gospel to its distilled essence and the methodization of the conversion process make widespread distribution of the gospel possible, while maintaining a cognitive uniformity in substantive quality of the message and an experiential uniformity in functional quality of the process. The packaging of the other dimensions of Evangelical spirituality produces similar effects.

That modern pluralistic societies bring the pressure of market competition to bear on belief systems is an academic commonplace (e.g., P. Berger, 1969; Wilson, 1976). Yet whereas a mostly passive ecumenicism has been the primary mode by which most faiths have dealt with this pressure, Evangelicalism has differed. Repudiating ecumenicism, it has opted for a strategy that begins by maintaining its own uniqueness and proceeds by reducing its singularity to easily grasped packages. Put differently, if belief systems are reduced in pluralistic societies to commodities from which people must choose, then Evangelicalism has responded, not by consolidating forces with other faiths, but by becoming packaged for easy, rapid, and strain-free consumption. Modernity puts all belief systems on the defensive. Evangelicalism is no exception. A central, though latent, function of the accommodation of Evangelical spirituality to the rationality of modernity, then, has been that the form of accommodation provides a strategy by which Evangelicals can aggressively contend with the strain brought about by cultural pluralism.

Cultural Plurality and the Rise of Evangelical Civility

In Chapter 2, I discussed the three options from which a person must choose when confronted with the dilemma of an intensive cultural and religious pluralism. He may decide that the claims of all religions are true, each representing different, though not antagonistic, perceptions of the same core reality. The converse is to decide that the claims of each religious belief system negate the others, making the claims of all religions necessarily false. The last option is cognitive intransigence: rejecting the truth claims of all other religions and maintaining the superiority of one's own. Evangelicalism as a socioreligious group of course falls into this last category. While it maintains an uncompromising position, it does not avoid the strains that a sustained contact with these forces engenders. There are subtle consequences of this encounter that appear only over time and that even an orthodoxy may find difficult to avoid.

At one level, the diversity of cultural traditions fosters a moral and ethical ambiguity. Under these circumstances, the existence of a clearly defined set of normative codes for a variety of life situations breaks down. In examining the survey data on a number of these moral and ethical issues, several interesting things come to light. Owing in large measure to their distance from the world-disaffirming structures and processes of modernity and their consequent ability to maintain traditional ethical standards, Evangelicals as a religious group are less affected by these pressures than other religious groups. From a review of Table 6.1, one may see that Evangelicals rank highest in their opposition to homosexuality (88.7%), premarital sexual intercourse (82.6%), and extramarital sexual intercourse (96.7%). They also rank highest in their opposition to divorce except under certain circumstances (66.7%) and to abortion (95.3%) with the exception of therapeutic abortion (abortion when the mother's life is in danger). Overall, Catholics rank second and liberal Protestants third.

Table 6.2 concerns the manner in which respondents view their ethical and moral standards. Evangelicals reveal the least amount of confusion (4.9%) or fatalism (6.7%) about their ability to live up to their ethical and

TABLE 6.1

"IMMORAL BEHAVIOR" BY RELIGIOUS PREFERENCE (in percentages)

	Evangelical	Liberal	Catholic	Non-Christian	Secularist
Homosexuality	88.7	70.3	68.6	43.8	40.9
Premarital relations	82.6	51.7	54.1	22.9	15.8
Extramarital relations	96.7	88.6	88.8	74.0	64.4
Abortion	95.3	85.5	90.5	42.6	68.0
Divorce	66.7	47.0	57.4	30.9	20.9
N =	(347)	(540)	(474)	(56)	(132)

TABLE 6.2

VIEWS OF MORAL STANDARDS BY RELIGIOUS PREFERENCE (in percentages)

	Evangelical	Liberal	Catholic	Non-Christian	Secularist
My standards are *ideal* standards that I never really expect to achieve.
	8.9	5.4	5.9	9.6	4.6
Most of the time I am able to live up to my moral and ethical standards.
	55.9	60.0	57.5	71.2	51.9
I'm trying to live up to my moral and ethical standards but just find it hard to do so. It's something like the old saying, "The spirit is willing, but the flesh is weak."
	23.6	14.4	17.5	3.8	13.9
There is so much in today's culture that works against my standards that I often find it impossible to live up to what I think is right.
	6.7	8.4	8.5	9.6	14.8
I am often confused as to what is right and what isn't. One set of standards doesn't seem to fit every situation.
	4.9	11.8	10.6	5.8	14.8
	100.0	100.0	100.0	100.0	100.0
N =	(347)	(540)	(474)	(56)	(132)

moral standards. Yet they, among all the religious persuasions polled, have
the most difficulty in the struggle to live up to their standards (23.6%).
Although most Evangelicals (55.9%) claim to be able to live up to their
standards most of the time, they rank fourth highest among the religious
groups on this dimension. Finally, 8.9 percent of all Evangelicals claim
that their standards are ideals unlikely to be achieved. From this breakdown
one might infer that Evangelicals have a clearer notion of what is ethically
proper yet that these standards make more rigorous demands, causing Evangelicals to have the greatest difficulty of the religious groups in living up to
their standards.

Despite high resistance to accommodating to modern liberal moral tolerance, Evangelicals lack unanimity on all of the specific issues measured,
most notably homosexuality, premarital sexual relations, and divorce, as
Table 6.2 shows. Thus the pervasive moral ambiguity of the modern culture
has had some effect on the Evangelical subculture. Even among Evangelicals, traditional moral values have begun to lose certainty. For a small
though significant percentage of Evangelicals, homosexuality, premarital
sexual intercourse, and divorce are viable options.

The encounter with cultural pluralism has other consequences as well. As
I have said, the fundamental strain that pluralism produces at the level of
consciousness is the pressure to be tolerant, if not accepting, of those who
hold different beliefs. Yet it is this pressure that is so contrary to the doctrinal beliefs of Evangelicalism. For Evangelicalism to remain an orthodoxy,
it must, among other things, maintain its rigid monopolistic claims on religious truth. From the Evangelical perspective, the issue is clear-cut: orthodox Protestantism is the only true faith, and all other faiths are either de-
viations or manifestly false—the tools of Satanic deception. Put differently,
one is either saved or damned. The deciding factor in one's eternal fate is
whether one has faith in Jesus Christ to forgive sins or not. Those who believe in Jesus Christ as Savior will be saved from their sins and enter into
everlasting glory when they die; those who do not will perish for their sins
in the everlasting torment of the fires of hell. Contemporary American
Evangelicalism maintains this position as its cutting edge.

In a society in which an attitude of social and religious tolerance is not
only normatively defined but legally prescribed, extreme exclusivism such as
this is typically met with more than a distant sneer; it usually engenders
hostility and rage. Intolerance is not tolerated. But this is not the case at all
with contemporary Evangelicalism. On the contrary, contemporary Evangelicalism is not only tolerated but, even more surprising, often celebrated
both publicly and privately. This paradox poses a serious question: how is it
that so exclusivistic a group can experience such broadly based social acceptance in any modern society?

An answer is to be found in a historical shift in Evangelicalism's cultural demeanor. This has entailed a softening and a polishing of the more hard-line and barbed elements of the orthodox Protestant world view. Although at its doctrinal core this world view remains essentially unchanged, it has been culturally edited to give it the qualities of sociability and gentility. It has acquired a civility that proclaims loudly, "No offense, I am an Evangelical." Interesting in its own right, this shift is relevant here because it has resulted from a modified accommodation to the cultural plurality of modernity.

Christianity has not always been so civil. Its beginning was characterized by a social devisiveness, that left a trail of social and cultural (not to mention political) turmoil. Christianity from the post-Constantinian era through the Middle Ages was also marked by intolerance of religious dissenters (heretics). The centuries of the Reformation, Counter-Reformation, and Post-Reformation must be regarded similarly. Should one fail to mention the slaughter of German Anabaptists, the persecution of French Huguenots, the Spanish Inquisition, and the religious wars of the sixteenth and seventeenth centuries? Indeed, until the late nineteenth and early twentieth centuries, Christianity (Protestantism included) has been characterized by a rough-hewn, stern, and ungracious quality. Religious belief has always been regarded with utmost gravity and hence has always had serious consequences for social relations. Though often for the most unspiritual of motives, these consequences have typically led to a social discourse of incivility if not beastiality among those with contrary beliefs. Among liberal Protestants, the turn toward civility as a mode of social discourse began with the drive in church polity toward ecumenicism. Conservative Protestantism as a whole remained characterized in the popular imagination as stern and ill-mannered until the early 1940s. Then the repudiation of the "bad manners" of separatist Fundamentalism by the NAE in 1942 established a pattern that was to become dominant in all major sectors of conservative Protestantism in America—the trend toward civility. Christianity, even in the most intransigent quarters, has become "civil."

Civility is most noticeable when those who have already accepted the Evangelical message interact with those being introduced to it. The civilizing process entails a deemphasis of Evangelicalism's more offensive aspects: the notions of inherent evil, sinful conduct and lifestyles, the wrath of a righteous and jealous God, and eternal agony and death in hell. This deemphasis has been more quantitative than qualitative. The offensive elements are, in the main, neither substantively devalued nor glossed over as unimportant. They are simply not referred to as much as they have been in the past. These elements have not lost their doctrinal centrality but have lost a stylistic centrality once taken for granted in the preaching and teaching in this tradition. "Sin," Kennedy (1977) instructs, "is a touchy matter" (p. 182). So too are the matters of judgment and hell. Of these delicate subjects, sin is discussed more openly than the others. Discussions of it can be found in all of the literature dealing with communicating the gospel. The definition of sin employed is traditional. It is understood as an individual dilemma, not an institutional one or a combination of both.

Nonetheless, sin discussed at this level is typically abstract. Rarely is the term used directly in the accusative manner common to the style of Cotton Mather, Jonathan Edwards, Finney, Moody, and Billy Sunday. Illustrative of the awareness Evangelicals have of the offensive nature of the notion of sin and their consequent ambivalence toward its use in public dialogue is a passage from the evangelism training manual, *Evangelism Explosion* (Kennedy, 1977):

> Is there any way to get the point across that a person is a sinner without making him unnecessarily angry at us? The portion of the gospel presentation dealing with the fact that man is a sinner and cannot save himself is one place where prospects can sometimes get a little bit disturbed with us. (p. 182)

There follows a method for dealing with the issue.

What is more pronounced than the mode in which sin is discussed is the lack of discussion of the consequences of sin, namely, an eschatological judgment, damnation, and the eternal torment and anguish of hell. While it is possible to be academic about sin, it is much more difficult to be so with the terms *eternal damnation* and *hell*. As a result, they are rarely mentioned in the literature or in public sermons except by vague reference or implication. In the *Four Spiritual Laws* tract (Bright, 1965) and other Campus Crusade literature, the terms *hell* and *damnation* are not used at all but replaced with the more genteel *perish*. This pattern is followed in the literature of other evangelistic organizations as well, the Billy Graham Evangelistic Organization in particular. When the specific consequences of sin are mentioned, they are often preceded with an apology. Graham in *How To Be Born Again* (1977) is representative of this tendency: "Crime requires punishment and sin has a penalty. Although this may be a subject we would like to ignore, it is an unavoidable fact. Not only does everyone suffer as a result of sin in this life, but everyone must face the judgement to come. . . . The third dimension of death is eternal death. This may be a subject which most try to avoid. We hear a lot about 'hell on earth,' but there is another hell which is more real and certain, and that's the hell of eternal death" (pp. 87, 90).

This marks a major shift from the time when long and detailed descriptions of hell were preached to congregations and impromptu crowds alike. As every evangelist and preacher knew, the horror and dread of such a fate provided not only a means for social control in the community but, even more fundamentally, the primary motive for becoming a convert in the first place. People became Christians largely because they were terrified of an eternity in hell. This leads to a second quality of Evangelical civility.

As civility has entailed a deemphasis of the negative aspects of the Protestant world view, it has also meant the accentuation of the positive. Evangelizing techniques repeatedly encourage what they call a "positive and exciting presentation of the gospel" message. This may at first seem nothing new (after all, Christ preached a positive and exciting message), but the "good news" preached formerly was other-worldly in essence. The excitement communicated on the contemporary scene is almost exclusively inner-worldly.

Each of the four spiritual laws outlined in the Campus Crusade for Christ tract centers around "God's love and wonderful plan for our lives." Even Graham (1977) has stressed the positive inner-worldly benefits of belief before the negative consequences of unbelief: "Levels of living we have never attained await us. Peace, satisfaction, and joy we have never experienced are available to us" (p. 33). Kennedy's evangelism training manual (1977) encourages trainees to "stress the positive benefits of the gospel" (p. 111). Rather than using the threat of hell as a pique to conversion, Kennedy says, one should "simply tell them about the wonders of eternal life which Christ gives" (p. 49). Other "motives for receiving eternal life" are that God:

> Provides us with Christian fellowship and friends.
> He fills us with his love.
> He forgives us and relieves our sense of guilt.
> He adopts us into his family.
> He gives us a whole new perspective on life.
> He delivers us from the fears of living or dying. (p. 74 f.)

In each case the orientation is away from an other-worldly despair and toward an inner-worldly goodness, the latter, of course, being the least offensive approach.

Even the fairly recent adoption of the born-again motif that characterizes the Evangelical conversion experience and the contemporary movement at large has had consequences in this regard. At the societal level, it has provided the movement with what can be viewed as an exciting and optimistic public relations theme. It is a theme even the most devout Jew or sensitive agnostic would not find offensive. At the microsocial level it has similar consequences. The term *born-again* implicitly requires a sustained dramaturgy among all those who claim it as their own. It is a dramaturgy that includes the continued expression of joy, happiness, peace of mind, satisfaction, and optimism about life. This presentation of self is a rudimentary characteristic of the public image of Evangelicalism.

In the aforementioned evangelistic training manuals and in Campus Crusade literature on evangelism, the language and demeanor of civility and its centrality in communicating the gospel are described:

> Don't carry a large Bible on your [evangelistic] visit. A large Bible can have
> the same effect as a .45 revolver. (Kennedy, 1977:111)
> Do look sharp—well groomed—confident. (Sisson, 1979:144)

Watch your grooming and manner of dress. (Kennedy, 1977:112)

Ask a friend if you have bad breath . . . do something to get rid of it. (Kennedy, 1977:112)

[Make] a cordial and friendly greeting. (Bright, 1971:no.6, p. 39)

Don't start your gospel presentation until tensions ease and both parties relax. (Sisson, 1979:144)

Humor at this point can cause them to relax and change their whole attitude. (Kennedy, 1977:48)

Pay him a sincere compliment. (Kennedy, 1977:51)

Don't criticize his denomination, his congregation, his minister, or him as a person. (Kennedy, 1977:51 f.)

When you have convinced your listeners that you are friendly and genuinely interested in their family, they will begin to relax. (Sisson, 1979:144)

If the answers to the diagnostic questions are wrong, tell the person that he is wrong without making him angry. (Kennedy, 1977:50)

Ask permission to share the gospel. (Kennedy, 1977:49)

Do not try to badger, argue, or high pressure him into making a "decision for Christ." (Bright, 1971:no. 6, p. 39)

Don't use high pressure tactics if a person is hesitant to make a decision. (Sisson, 1979:150)

High pressure tactics are to be abhorred. (Kennedy, 1977:112)

[We must] learn to expose our faith, not impose it. (Pippert, 1979:129)

Do smile, especially as you ask the two commitment questions. If you are too intense, your prospect may feel he is being pinned down, and resent it. (Kennedy, 1977:112)

When we explain the Christian message, we should learn to do so in plain language. . . . few things turn off people faster or alienate them more easily than God-talk. (Pippert, 1979:130)

Do make your exit sweet—even if the gospel has been rejected. (Kennedy, 1977:112)

What perhaps best summarizes this approach is a comment by Bright (1971): "In making the presentation, show love. Be casual, friendly, warm and speak with confidence" (no. 6, p. 31). The meaning of Christian love is, therefore, largely redefined. In the popular imagination, it has come to be understood more in terms of the discourse and lifestyle of civility than as self-effacing and sacrificial giving. Parody often performs a didactic function by bringing out the irony of a situation. The highest act of Christian love as understood by the contemporary Evangelical could be parodied as the act of saying, "No offense, brother, but you're going to burn in hell if you don't repent and accept Jesus Christ as your personal Lord and Savior."[3]

Cultural pluralism places pressure on the adherents of a particular belief system to be accepting of those from other traditions. Evangelicalism has resisted accommodating to this pressure at the doctrinal level; it has made certain concessions at the level of social demeanor and social discourse.

To begin with, most Evangelicals tacitly recognize that Protestant hegemony in America has given way to a potpourri of religious belief systems that itself is girded by a strong liberal code of religious tolerance. Moreover, they tacitly accept this situation—that, for the time being, these are the conditions in which they will have to operate. In response, Evangelicalism has adopted a social posture that pleads, "Don't take offense, but here is the truth." It is a demeanor of propriety, gentility, and sociability. But Evangelicalism's modified accommodation to the cognitive constraints of pluralism has not been entirely passive. Often accommodation has been aggressively pursued. Civility as a mode of discourse provides an additional strategy for proffering beliefs and doctrine in market competition. On the one hand, it allows Evangelicalism to be perceived as being in "good taste,"—positive, and upbeat. On the other hand, it allows for a forum in which religious one-upmanship can take place smoothly, maintaining, not so much that Evangelical Christianity is more true than other faiths, but that Evangelical Christianity is superior to other faiths because of the superior (i.e., inner-worldly) benefits it provides: inner peace, true joy and happiness, dependable fellowship, and a source of strength in times of need, all in addition to an eternal life in heaven. Accommodation to modernity in this way has provided another curious twist to the heritage of conservative Protestantism in America.

Structural Plurality: Subjectivization and the New Theodicy

Institutional differentiation and segmentation and the resulting bifurcation of social experience into public and private spheres has decisive consequences for religious world views. Structural pluralization creates a situation that limits the relevance of religious symbols and meaning to certain sectors of social experience. At the level of consciousness there is pressure for religion to become relevant only within the private sphere, that of family, intimate social relations, and the self, not in the public sphere, the state most notably. Is Evangelical faith primarily a private experience? Has it become depoliticized or does it retain a public, even political, edge? Although the answer is not clear-cut, it is probably both. Evangelicalism has become privatized in some ways, but in other ways it has resisted privatization in favor of a bold political prowess. The nature of the political side of contemporary Evangelicalism, I leave for another chapter. What is of concern here is the manner in which the Evangelical world view has accommodated to the pressures toward privatization and the qualitative differences this makes in this world view.[4]

On privatization, the survey data reveal some interesting things. Confirming the conjecture that Evangelicals do retain a public dimension is their score on the privatization scale (see Table 6.3). Evangelicals rank highest

TABLE 6.3

PRIVATIZATION SCALE

	Number	Mean value score	Standard deviation	Standard error
Evangelicals	310	5.23	2.08	0.118
Liberals	483	6.79	2.42	0.110
Catholics	427	6.46	2.29	0.111
Non-Christians	51	8.43	2.69	0.38
Secularists	107	8.29	2.87	0.277
	1,378	6.52	2.52	0.678

Note. This scale was constructed by assigning numerical values to the value categories of three variables—importance of religious organizations stating what they believe to be the will of God in (1) ethical and moral matters, (2) spiritual and religious matters, and (3) political and economic matters—and then tallying scores for each respondent. The value categories and their assigned values were the same for each variable: strongly agree (1), agree (2), disagree (3), and strongly disagree (4). Thus, the higher the score, the more privatized the respondent's religious orientation. Conversely, the lower the score, the less private—more public—the view. Minimum score = 3; maximum = 12. Alpha coefficient: 0.7417.

Source	df	Sum of squares	Mean squares	F Rating	F Probability
Between groups	4	1,077.6341	269.41	48.43	0.00
Within groups	1,373	7,638.4924	5.63		
Total	1,377	8,716.1250			

(i.e., they had the lowest average score in the value-assignment poll) in their belief that religious organizations should make public statements about the will of God on ethical and moral matters, spiritual and religious matters, and political and economic matters. In this they differ significantly from all other religious groups. Catholics ranked second, liberal Protestants third; secularists, ranked fourth, did not differ significantly from non-Christians, who are the most privatized of all religious groups.

Yet the survey data can only be a prolegomenon, for it does not reveal the more subtle and qualitative dimensions of the problem of privatization. It has been argued that subjectivization (the structural process of being forced to turn inward to find meaningful life patterns and a stable identity) fosters subjectivism, an orientation marked not so much by vanity as by an incessant preoccupation with the hitherto "undiscovered" complexities of one's individual subjectivity. An institutional process directing one into the self leads to the preoccupation with the self, and this bears on the issue of the privatization of religion in a peculiar way.

All religions attempt to make sense of the anomie endemic to individual and social existence in the world, for this is the task of theodicy. Yet a change has occurred. The sphere of problems for which a theodicy must account has been expanded. Beyond the conventional problems of physical suffering, grief, death, and the spiritual state of man, a religious theodicy under the conditions of modernity must deal with a new set of problems. In different terms, religion in modern society is under pressure to remain institutionally and symbolically sequestered in the private sphere; at the same time the complexities of experience in the private sphere expand. Religion, qua meaning system, is faced with more problems with which to reconcile to its adherents: those of subjectivism. A religious theodicy in the modern situation is presented with the task of accounting for and addressing the new and uncharted complexities of the self and all the problems involved in the "new mental health."[5]

Accommodation to structural pluralism, then, has largely come to mean the degree to which a religious world view becomes entangled in the thicket of intrasubjectivity. Contemporary American Evangelicalism is presented with precisely this situation. Like all other faiths in the modern situation, it faces structural constraints to become engrossed in the endless mire of intrasubjective musings. It is not surprising, then, that Evangelicalism has yielded to these constraints in some significant ways. The plethora of popular Evangelical literature that emerged in the 1960s and especially in the 1970s to deal with such phenomena is evidence of this accommodation. A topical review of the books of eight major publishers of popular Evangelical literature (Appendix 2) showed that 12.3 percent of all titles fell into a category defined by the orientation toward understanding or explaining the emotional and psychological complexities of human experience from an Evangelical perspective. The range for this category was between 7.2 percent (Bethany) and 19.9 percent (Gospel Light), with the average percentage of the entire sample being 13.9 percent. What is important is not simply that this category has such a significant percentage relative to other categories; it is that the category exists at all for conservative Protestants.

Starting with the invention of the printing press, the publication efforts of dedicated Protestants went almost exclusively into Bibles, mass books, and catechisms. Considerably less effort went into the publication of theological tracts, treatises, and devotional material. This remained true until the nineteenth century, when more energies went into the publication of theological tracts and apologetic treatises in defense of an increasingly beleaguered faith. Most of this literature was oriented toward a literate elite and quasi-elite. The publication of Bibles has remained a central task among conservative Protestant publishers to the present. Yet since the postwar era, great efforts have gone into developing a high-volume market of literature addressing the needs and shaping the perspectives of the man on the street. Only recently has literature been published with titles such as *God's Psychiatry* (Allen, 1953), *The Sensation of Being Somebody: Building an Adequate Self-Concept* (Wagner, 1979), *Search for Reality*, (Collins, 1969), or *The Art of Get-*

ting Along with People (Osborne, 1980), reflecting a unique subjectivism in the Evangelical world view. A closer examination is warranted.

Underlying Evangelicalism's accommodation to subjectivism is the acceptance of the legitimacy of the modern question Who am I? (P. Berger, 1976; P. Berger et al., 1974; Turner, 1976). The question is only comprehensible in a society in which identity has become deinstitutionalized. The self has become a boundaryless territory to be explored, analyzed, and mapped, an exercise that often requires the assistance of "experts." Evangelicalism affirms this enterprise as legitimate and has produced its own experts. One book invites readers to "explore yourself and to know yourself perhaps more deeply than you have explored or known before" (Kilgore, 1977:15); at the same time: "self-exploration is like eating one potato chip. If you start, it is likely that you cannot quit. This is the bridge of no return" (p. 16).

This type of self-examination goes beyond the traditional Christian pietistic exercise of searching heart and soul, a predominantly spiritual exercise oriented around one's concern for one's spiritual condition (e.g., the rule of sin in life and the process of mortification and sanctification). Reflection directed toward spiritual mastery remains an Evangelical concern, but contemporary Evangelicalism differs from traditional Protestantism in the added, central concern with the emotional and psychological dimensions of human experience.

One dimension of this orientation is an emphasis on achieving "psychological balance" and "emotional maturity." Careful examination of titles in the broad category of books on emotional and psychological problems reveals that the specific problem of balance, maturity, and self-actualization is the most important (see Table 6.4). Of all of these books, 32.5 percent fall into this subcategory. Examples of such books are: *God's Key to Health and Happiness* (Josephson, 1976); *Transformed Temperaments* (LaHaye, 1981);

TABLE 6.4

EVANGELICAL LITERATURE CONCERNED WITH EMOTIONAL AND
PSYCHOLOGICAL PROBLEMS BY PUBLISHER (in percentages)

	Bethany	Gospel Light	Moody
Emotional/psychological problems	23.1	34.6	44.4
Traditional theodicy	0.0	11.5	25.9
Emotional/psychological balance	30.8	11.5	18.6
Hedonism/narcissism	46.1	42.4	11.1
	100.0	100.0	100.0
N =	(13)	(26)	(27)

The Art of Understanding Yourself (Osborne, 1968); *Faith, Psychology and Christian Maturity* (Sall, 1977); *Mental Health: A Christian Approach* (Cosgrove and Mallory, 1977); *Psychology of Jesus and Mental Health* (Cramer, 1980); *You Can Change Your Personality* (Bustanby, 1977); and *Do I Have To Be Me?* (Ahlem, 1973).

These analyses differ in degree of sophistication. At one level there is the crude psychologizing of biblical language and imagery—making the Bible relevant to the intrasubjective queries of modern man. An example of this is found in Allen's *God's Psychiatry* (1953), where he shows how the Lord's Prayer, the Beatitudes, and other selected portions of the Bible provide guidelines for modern living. At the highest level, there is the synthesis of biblicism and humanistic or Freudian psychology. Here, the language of this perspective (e.g., awareness, assessment, self-actualization) is provided a biblical basis and given a spiritual relevance. Thus, these works also differ on substantive grounds. Yet the substantive difference is superficial, for what they all share is a *psychological Christocentrism*—a view of authentic mental and emotional health as rooted in the "establishment of a harmonious relationship with God through Jesus Christ," for "only God really transforms." This Christocentrism would of course be expected of Evangelicals.

A closely related dimension of this orientation is the emphasis on understanding and solving specific emotional and psychological problems. Such human experiences as guilt, anxiety, depression, stress, and tension are all included in this category. Once again, the literature review suggests the importance of such problems in the Evangelical world view. Of all books reviewed, 27.4 percent dealt with the "new" mental health problems as compared with 12.2 percent of all books chiefly concerned with the articulation of a traditional theodicy. Popular titles such as *Release from Tension* (Adolph, 1956); *I Want Happiness, Now!* (Brandt, 1978); *Defeating Despair and Depression* (Nordtvedt, 1976); *This Way to Happiness* (Narramore, 1969); *Why*

Revell/Spire	Scripture	Tyndale	Word	Zondervan	Total
14.8	13.0	40.0	29.2	21.6	27.4
7.4	8.7	10.0	8.3	16.2	12.2
37.0	60.9	25.0	41.7	35.2	32.5
40.8	17.4	25.0	20.8	27.0	27.9
100.0	100.0	100.0	100.0	100.0	100.0
(27)	(23)	(20)	(24)	(37)	(197)

Christians Crack Up (Nelson, 1974); *How To Handle Pressure* (Narramore
and Narramore, 1975); *How To Get through Your Struggles* (Roberts, 1978);
You Can Prevent a Nervous Breakdown (Caldwell, 1978); *You and Your
Husband's Mid-life Crisis* (Conway, 1980); *Feeling Good about Feeling Bad*
(Eggum, 1979); *Relax and Live Longer* (Collins, 1977); *How To Win over
Depression* (LaHaye, 1974); and *How To Win over Worry* (Haggai, 1967)
provide clear examples of this tendency. One explanation for this ascendancy
of the new mental health problems over the problems dealt with by a traditional theodicy in literature is that the solution to the problem of death
is already taken for granted by most Evangelicals. Furthermore, the absence
of intense physical suffering from severe economic conditions or harsh political or religious persecutions also reduces the traditional scope of theodicy.

In the assessing and addressing of such perplexities as worry, tension,
depression, and loneliness, there is also diversity in the literature, yet among
popular Evangelical psychologists there is agreement on the source of these
experiences. Ultimately, subjective dissension is traceable to sin, generic (the
sinful condition of mankind) and specific (the sins of the individual). It is
commonly said that "if man were not separated from God and still experienced communion with Him, then man would not experience these problems." Naturally, popular Evangelical psychologists are careful to discuss at
length the physiological and psychological sources of these experiences in
addition to their spiritual sources. Yet they regard the theological foundation as paramount.

Most modern people have an experiential understanding of these problems;
what they lack is a means for coping with them. Thus the emphasis in this
literature is on effective measures for dealing with such problems. The foundation, as one would expect, is spiritual. Guilt as an everyday experience
is based on spiritual guilt:

> Man's conscience re-echoes the condemnation—"all have sinned." . . .
> Guilt and sin are too big for man to cope with. But he doesn't need to.
> Christ has already paid the penalty. . . . God does not promise escape
> from every fearful situation, but He does promise to walk with us through
> every experience! And we can be strong and unafraid because God is the
> strength of our life. (Narramore, 1969:38, 43, 103)

Tension and stress? "The way back to peace of mind is through confession,
turning to Christ and walking daily with Him" (Narramore, 1969:107).
"This is God's way of coping with stress: (1) Become a believer, (2) Don't
worry about anything, (3) Pray about everything, (4) Give thanks, (5) Medi-
tate, (6) Trust God, (7) Honor God's laws" (Sumrall, 1979:16). Depression?
"If you are a child of God, you have the capacity to live a depressed-
free life. That does not guarantee you will, but you possess the external
power that will enable you to do so" (LaHaye, 1974:87). Insecurity? "The

new birth brings with it renewed potential for self-esteem and thus self-confidence" (Sumrall, 1979:99). In general, it is agreed "that Christianity, conscientiously applied to the emotional tension problems of our era, offers [a] complete and satisfactory solution" (Adolph, 1956:15). Or in Narramore's (1969) words:

> Human techniques are not enough. At best, our wisdom and understanding are hampered by human limitations. Psychological needs met solely on this level are never met adequately. It is God who completely understands our basic needs. And He has made provision to meet them in ways far superior to man's. (p. 47)

Another important dimension of the accommodation to subjectivism is the orientation toward narcissism and hedonism, the latter an extension of the former. From enamoredness with the self easily comes the attitude that the world exists for the purpose of pampering the self with pleasure and enjoyment. In this, Evangelicalism's accommodation takes on a more distinctly American flavor. Although all modern societies structurally engender subjectivism, it is only in free societies that narcissistic and hedonistic attitudes can easily emerge.

The review of popular Evangelical literature suggests the centrality of this orientation in the world view of American Evangelicalism. Nearly 28 percent of all titles reviewed addressed one or more dimensions of this general attitude, with books explicating the hedonistic attitudes in the majority. Examples of such books are *Self-love* (Schuller, 1969), *You Can Become the Person You Want To Be* (Schuller, 1973), *The Gift of Joy* (Flynn, 1980), *Move Ahead with Possibility Thinking* (Schuller, 1979), *Dare To Live Now* (Larson, 1972), *Happiness: You Can Find the Secret* (Hubbard, 1976), *How To Be a Happy Christian* (Nieboer, 1953), and *How To Become Your Own Best Self* (Grimes, 1979), among others. These broad assertions need qualification.

The narcissism and hedonism Evangelicalism expresses are clearly different from those qualities in the broader American culture, where hedonism reaches its apex in the phrase "If it feels good, do it." The narcissism found among Evangelicals is expressed not as self-infatuation or vanity or unseemly conceit with personal accomplishments. Rather, it finds expression in a fixation on the potentiality of the human being "under the lordship of Jesus Christ." Typical are the following comments:

> You can become the person you want to be. (Schuller, 1973:15)
> You can become a wonderful and worthwhile person. (Schuller, 1969:13)
> Simply affirm, "Christ lives within me—so I am a wonderful person." (Schuller, 1969:108)

> [You] can be set free to become. That is what Jesus Christ's life—death—and
> re-life are all about. (Augsburger, 1970:18)
> And His Spirit can provide the creative strength to make life's understandings
> and misunderstandings sparkle with constructive growth, if we follow Him in
> all of life. (Augsburger, 1970:115)
> Because each human being is a person, bearing this likeness to the Creator,
> each person is special and important to God. You're special—and have always
> been special. (Richards, 1977:18)

The narcissistic quality of this perception of the individual is in sharp contrast to the relative inattention of Evangelicalism to the common welfare of
disadvantaged social groups and politically oppressed societies or even to the
spiritual well-being of the church as a whole.

Similarly, the hedonism found in the Evangelical world view is expressed
not in unbridled surfeit of material substance but in the conviction that
human experience should be characterized by unfathomable inner joy and
happiness and the unquenchable expectancy of good things. Bright (1971)
has noted that "Jesus meant for the Christian life to be an exciting, abundant
adventure. . . . A rich and satisfying life is the heritage of the Christian.
. . . But most Christians don't know anything about this kind of life—a
life of victory, joy and abundant fruitfulness for our Savior (no. 2, pp. 5, 6).
"We often ignore the fact that our heavenly Father has designed a plan to
make us happy and fulfilled, to help us grow into His mature children,"
according to T. Foster (1980:85). Cook (1978b) has said that Christ gives
"a new zest for living" (p. 86). Graham (1977) has written: "Levels of living
we have never attained await us. Peace, satisfaction, and joy we have never
experienced are available to us. God is trying to break through. The heavens
are calling and God is speaking" (p. 34). Flynn (1980) exhorts, "Godliness is
not gloom but gladness" (p. 26). The life missing these qualities is often
regarded as deficient, certainly as a life lived to less than its potential.
Within American Evangelicalism, if one is spiritual, one is happy and con-
tented. Life is full and rich. Conversely, the routine mediocrity of everyday
life, commonplace to most, is often considered a measure of the lack of
spirituality. In Evangelicalism such spiritual joy is tacitly considered not just
an inner quality but one that demands public expression. Even in the face
of extreme difficulties, the Evangelical often feels constrained to exhibit,
not just perseverance and fortitude, but happiness and joy. This can foster
a public dramaturgy unsupported by subjective conviction. Nonetheless, a
symmetry between public display and inner belief is regarded as normative.
Hedonism in this context, then, entails the public and subjective denial of
inner suffering, dread, and boredom as essential features of human existence.

All in all, while sharply circumscribed by what might be regarded as an
antiquated doctrinal code, Evangelicalism has nonetheless been able to

achieve through these modes of accommodation a contemporaneity of cultural expression that more or less succeeds in addressing the sensitivities and "needs" of modern man. As a result, Evangelical faith is more plausible, less objectionable, to him. Contemporaneity thus provides another strategy by which Evangelicals may more easily proffer their beliefs in the emporium of religious faiths.

Yet contemporaneity is not without its more dubious consequences. Subjectivism, which has culminated in narcissism and hedonism, has displaced the traditional asceticism as the dominant attitude in theologically conservative Protestant culture. There is some variability, but in mainstream contemporary American Evangelicalism, an austere instrumentalism has been replaced by a malleable expressivity. The inner posture of mastery of ascetic Protestantism has given way to an inner flaccidity of a largely subjectivistically oriented Evangelicalism. Thus accommodation to the constraints of structural pluralism has added yet another curious historical twist to the tradition of conservative Protestantism in America.

Conclusions

Few religious groups in contemporary America claim the title of orthodoxy when referring to their own religious beliefs. To lay such a claim, as the term denotes, is to maintain that one's religious beliefs conform strictly to the doctrines and creeds established during the primitive era of one's religious tradition. The rigor of the term precludes its casual employment as a self-descriptive adjective. Yet American Evangelicals constitute one group bold enough to use the term in such a manner. Evangelicalism is widely held to have a direct theological lineage from the apostolic age and the Reformation, the latter being the major historical reaffirmation of apostolic belief in Western history.

Given Evangelicalism's accommodation to modernity, can it seriously maintain its claim of falling in the line of orthodox succession? Doctrinally, it still does, with the few exceptions discussed earlier. Yet while the doctrinal creed of conservative Protestantism has remained largely unchanged by the encounter with modernity, the cognitive style has changed, and changed in significant ways.

An important consequence of Evangelicalism's accommodation to modernity has been its increased marketability in a highly competitive religious market place. The packaging of Evangelical spirituality has made it easy to adopt. The civility of the contemporary Evangelical message makes it less objectionable to nonbelievers. The subjectivization of Evangelical faith allows it to be "more relevant" to the needs and perspectives of modern man. Such changes indeed have proved "successful." Yet the most notable consequence of the accommodation to modernity has been the domestication of conservative Protestant belief.

The rationalization of the conversion experience and all other dimensions of Evangelical spirituality has had the effect of harnessing the ecstatic, taming the unpredictable, and pacifying the "unruly" qualities of Evangelical faith. When the truly charismatic areas of religious experience are rigorously defined, systematized, and cataloged, the religion is divested of a non-empirical energy and force necessary to sustain it over time. In great measure this describes the present situation of American Evangelicalism. Spiritual experience has largely become domesticated as a result of the rationalization of spirituality. The full consequences are probably yet to be revealed.

To claim orthodoxy is to imply that all others are heterodox. Yet while Evangelicalism maintains an orthodox exclusivism, the cry "heresy!" is never publicly and rarely privately uttered by Evangelicals. Such "fanaticism" has been tempered by "good sense"; such "zeal" is moderated by "reasonableness and propriety." Evangelical belief has lost its rough-hewn quality, which has been replaced by gentility. The limited accommodation to cultural plurality has therefore also resulted in a domestication of Evangelical faith.

Finally, the contemporaneity that Evangelicalism achieves through its accommodation to modern subjectivism has had the effect of weakening the asceticism characteristic of Protestantism in earlier periods. The "hardness" that results from the certainty concerning one's experience in the world and one's relation to an other-worldly reality is replaced by a "softness" that arises in a milieu of personal and social ambiguity. Evangelicalism has attempted to deal with such ambiguity neither by ignoring it nor by encouraging the quiet retreat of Evangelicals into sociocultural enclaves where social ambiguity will present no problems but rather by accepting its validity and dealing with it as a legitimate problem. As spiritual exercises, self-discipline and self-denial are hardly conceivable in a situation where the nature of that which is to be denied and disciplined is under constant examination. The narcissism and hedonism evidenced in Evangelicalism only accentuates the "soft" character of the Evangelical world view. To the degree that Puritan asceticism becomes displaced by subjectivism and its attendant cultural by-products, Evangelical faith becomes domesticated that much further.

The phrase "cooperation without compromise" originally referred to a political posture for Evangelicals dealing with nonconservative Protestants and Protestant organizations. It could be reasonably argued that it aptly described a social posture as well, for dealing with "the world." What Evangelicals did not know in the early 1940s was that, sociologically, cooperation inevitably necessitates compromise. While Evangelicalism has not thrown in the doctrinal or theological towel, as it were, it has conceded a great deal in its encounter with modernity. At this point the concessions have largely been cultural. The cognitive style of the Evangelical world view is substantially different from what it had been. Put descriptively, the old-style nineteenth-century Evangelical, rigidly ascetic, brashly intolerant of other faiths, and somewhat irrational about his approach to spiritual life, has given way to the new-style Evangelical, technical about his faith, civilly intolerant with those of other faiths, and contemporary. These patterns are especially dominant among those Evangelicals who are in the higher echelons of education and income. Whether this cultural accommodation will eventually result in a doctrinal compromise remains to be seen. Given the concessions that have already been made, the larger question that remains to haunt Evangelicalism is what will be the longer term effects of its encounter with modernity.

7

Resistances: Public Piety and Politization

The concessions Evangelicalism has made to modernity are not the entire story. Evangelicalism has remained shrewdly reluctant to gamble away all of its treasures for the sake of being contemporaneous. Indeed, as I have noted, the dominant trait of its history from the late nineteenth century has been an aggressive resistance to the constraints of modernity; and with the exception of the concessions discussed in Chapter 6, Evangelicalism has maintained this posture to the present. Evangelicals, for example, have openly resisted constraints of rationality to reduce or explain away the supernatural or spiritual in terms of naturalistic categories. They have also resisted the pressures of cultural pluralism to abandon their exclusivism. Finally, they have resisted the pressures of structural pluralism to contain the significance of their religious symbols within the narrow boundaries of the private sphere. But Evangelicalism's resistance to modernity is much more complex than this, and the problems go much deeper. Modernity for the Evangelical has become a political problem.

Deinstitutionalization causes definitions of reality in the social world to become less generally accepted. Their coherence and credibility is undermined. Their truth or usefulness then becomes a matter of individual choice. Historically, the processes of deinstitutionalization are often differentially distributed. For various reasons, some parts of a world view will undergo these processes, while other parts avoid them for a time, and so it is with American Evangelicalism. There has been a historical lag between the deinstitutionalization of the specifically religious and spiritual dimensions of the conservative Protestant world view and the deinstitutionalization or erosion of the legitimacy of what Evangelicals regard as a Christian system of morality.

Religious and spiritual deinstitutionalization took place toward the end of the nineteenth century and through the first two decades of the twentieth, and it was against this process that Fundamentalism so vigorously struggled.

102

The tussles with theological liberalism, ecclesiastical and doctrinal ecumenism, and evolution in the classroom all exemplify the struggle against this process or, in the reverse, the endeavor to maintain Fundamentalism's cultural dominance. Though the religious cosmology of conservative Protestantism continued to be besieged through the first half of the twentieth century, the traditional morality of the nineteenth century remained essentially intact. Values such as premarital chastity, marital fidelity, the undesirability of divorce, and the sanctity of life all remained strongly institutionalized in the mainstream of American culture. The deinstitutionalization of this morality only began to gain momentum after World War II. Yet it was not until the mid-1960s and the 1970s that these processes began to accelerate. The increasing rates of divorce, the popularity of innovative courtship patterns (such as living together), the rise of permissive sexual mores (the so-called sexual revolution) and divergent "sexual lifestyles" (the gay rights movement), the usurpation of traditional gender roles (with the feminist movement), and the increasing acceptability of abortion on demand, all demonstrate the increasing deinstitutionalization of this traditional morality. It is against these forces in American culture that conservative Protestantism presently strives.

The Moral Decline of American Society

The threat to traditional morality that modernity poses is certainly ominous from the Evangelical perspective. To many, the fate of America and indeed Western civilization hinges on how American society deals with this threat. The dilemma, in the Evangelical mind, is not broad and undefined but shaped by specific issues.[1] Most of the threat is directed toward the private sphere. One particularly sensitive problem is legalized abortion. With the 1973 Supreme Court decision to legalize abortion came wide reaction from the American religious community in general. While the American Catholic community has been most vocal in opposing this decision, Evangelicalism has provided a strong populist base of opposition. As survey data has shown, it is not simply that abortion in all but the most extreme circumstances is seen as morally unacceptable by the overwhelming majority of Evangelicals. These attitudes translate into opinions on public policy. A notably larger percentage of Evangelicals (41%) than non-Evangelicals (25%) favor a ban on *all* abortions (Gallup, 1980c). Like the Catholics, Evangelicals typically regard the unborn fetus at any stage as a human being with all the rights of a citizen. Because God gives conception and creates each child, abortion is murder; and murder is sin. "In America, a Christian nation, we are killing one million of God's created people every year" (Price, 1976:92). Jesse Helms, senator from North Carolina, has articulated the surprise and the concern of Evangelicals over the deinstitutionalization of traditional "prolife" mores: "It still astonishes many people that abortion—and what is even more wide-spread, the toleration of abortion—has so quickly become an accomplished fact in the U.S." (Helms, 1976:68). Evangelicals have a long-range concern as well: "Will God continue to bless a nation that kills its babies?" (Price, 1976:86).

Another threat is posed by the feminist movement in America and its most important legislative proposal, the Equal Rights Amendment to the Constitution. From the Evangelical perspective, the feminist movement has brought about the de facto "undermining of God's line of authority in the home" (Billings, 1980b:3); the ERA, among other things, would bring about the de jure undermining of this structure and therefore threatens the future of the American family. National opinion polls show that the ERA is not nearly as important to the majority of Evangelicals as are other issues; roughly the same number approve of it as oppose it. Nonetheless, fewer Evangelicals (53%) than non-Evangelicals (66%) support the adoption of this amendment (Gallup, 1980c). Apart from this issue, it is widely held (implicitly or explicitly) in mainstream Evangelical circles that the "wife and mother has a holy calling of God as homemaker" (Sweeting, 1974:13; cf. Walton, 1975:95). Legally sanctioning and encouraging the role of women in the working world, because it "attacks the stability of the house," only contributes to the "disintegration of the family. [Indeed] the Equal Rights Amendment strikes at the foundation of our entire social structure" (Falwell, 1980b:251).

An additional problem is the "increasing degeneration" of all sexual mores: "In the 1960s and 1970s sex went public. Movies and magazines became sexually explicit. Best selling books abounded on the joy of sex. Shops selling pornographic materials proliferated. Homosexuals came out of the closet" (Kroll, 1980:16). Evangelicals are nearly unanimous in their opinion that premarital and extramarital sexual relations are morally unacceptable—an opinion on which there is greater consensus among Evangelicals than among any other large religious community in America (see Table 6.1). They also view this type of sexual license as on the increase. In the Evangelical view, these sexual practices, besides being a sin against God, are responsible for increased rates of other morally dubious phenomena—divorce, teenage pregnancy, and abortion—for depravity breeds more depravity. Pornography only contributes to the problem: "Pornography is a cancer that is changing the character of our republic" (Falwell, 1981:69). Especially offensive to Evangelicals is homosexuality. Acknowledging the deinstitutionalization of prohibitions against homosexual activity, one writer lamented, "We have also seen a change in America in our attitudes and laws towards homosexuals. It's very fashionable to dismiss this growing problem by saying 'Well, they're just a little different from us,' or 'It's just a sickness, like tuberculosis, or something.' However, God said that it's not a sickness, it's a sin" (Price, 1976:77). Evangelicals are particularly opposed to government legislation (the Gay Rights Bill) that would in any way protect practicing homosexuals in the occupational world, the public school in particular. Only a small percentage of Evangelicals (15%) (notably smaller than the 31% of non-Evangelicals) favor proposals that would allow homosexuals to teach in public schools (Gallup, 1980c). According to television evangelist Falwell (1980a), "It's time to declare war on homosexuality and defeat this bill now."

Another threat to the Evangelical definition of social propriety comes with increased rates of divorce. Divorce is now much easier to obtain and therefore more widespread. The consequence, it is held, is always the breakup of the God-ordained family structure: "Our families are falling apart because we've lost the power that holds families together—God" (Price, 1976:105). This occurrence largely accounts for the crumbling of American society, believes evangelical lawyer Price (1976):

> We have crime, in large part due to youthful offenders. They commit crimes due to their lack of proper, balanced, godly upbringing. This springs from homes broken by adultery, alcohol, promiscuity, and other sins. These problems arise due to a lack of proper upbringing. The circle completes itself and always comes back to failure to put God first in the family. (p. 75)

The final threat comes from public education. The Supreme Court decision banning prayer in public schools is regarded by many Evangelicals as a major cause of wholesale breakdown of moral values in society. An overwhelming majority of Evangelicals (81%), as opposed to non-Evangelicals (54%), favor legislative proposals that would require prayer in public schools (Gallup, 1980c). Helms (1976) noted:

> It is hardly coincidence that the banishment of the Lord from the public schools has resulted in their being taken over by a totally secularist philosophy. Christianity has been driven out. In its place has been enshrined a permissiveness in which the drug culture has flourished, as have pornography, crime, and fornication—in short, everything but disciplined learning. (p. 108)

Evangelical opinion in general maintains that the Supreme Court decision was based on a misreading of the First Amendment of the Constitution prohibiting the establishment of any one national religion by the Congress so that the right of freedom of religion would never be threatened. By legally prohibiting prayer from school, they argue, the Supreme Court "violated the establishment clause of the First Amendment by establishing a religion—the religion of secularism" (Helms, 1976:109).

Acknowledging the erosion of the credibility of all traditional moral structures in recent history, Falwell (1980b) has said, "Today we tolerate, laugh at, and even enjoy what twenty years ago would have deeply shocked us"

(p. 249). According to Walton (1975), "History attests that when morals decline and obscenity is glorified, nations are soon buried in their own debris" (p. 108; cf. Bright, 1976). The threat to traditional moral definitions is not limited to the private issues but extends to public-sphere, or "secular," issues. Inflation, for instance, is understood by many as a national sin arising from failure to apply God's economic guidelines (Walton, 1975:229–265). Inflation is sinful because "in printing money not backed by anything of material value—our government perpetrates a fraud and steals from the people" (Price, 1976:18). Helms (1976) believes "inflating the currency is tantamount to theft" (p. 60). Further, Evangelicals believe that the long-range consequences of government-spawned inflation will be the weakening of the American economy and the demoralization of the American spirit. The longevity of America as a Christian nation is imperiled as a result.

The threat is not only internal but external as well. A decline in America's defensive capabilities relative to the Soviet Union's military power is perceived widely in the Evangelical community: "The decline of America in the last handful of years is virtually unprecedented in world history" (Price, 1976:105). The Strategic Arms Limitation Treaties (and détente in general), the Panama Canal Treaty, and the loss of the Indo-China war are all perceived as significant events in the loss of American superiority in the international arena. Military superiority is regarded as essential to the peace and survival of the American way of life. More important, the survival of Christianity and Christian morality is linked to the survival of America; the longevity of Christianity largely depends on the relative strength of America (Walton, 1975:266–290).

Again, Evangelicalism is not monolithic on these issues. While Evangelicals of all traditions and social types tend to lament current patterns of moral change, they do not all express their concern similarly. Those with less education tend to be more separatist in their world view and as such are typically more vocal than those who have had more education and are less separatist. In terms of religious heritage, the Reformational-Confessional and the Anabaptist traditions on the whole (that is, apart from their intellectual spokespeople) tend to be less publically vocal in their critical assessment of present conditions. When vocal, Anabaptists, as one might expect, stand opposed to the course of conventional and strategic military build up in contrast to much of the Evangelical opinion on such matters. The Holiness-Pentecostal tradition, on the other hand, focuses its condemnation on the perceived deterioration of the private-sphere morality. Yet their complaint is typically directed internally (for the purpose of establishing distinct and reliable moral boundaries for its votaries) and not externally (to shame the secular world into a moral repentance). Without question, it is the Baptist tradition that is most publically vocal about its discontent. It is partly because of the current demographic and ideological dominance of the Baptist tradition in American Evangelicalism that the foregoing description of the moral threats does represent the general perception of a broad consensus of opinion on these issues.

The Evangelical complaint and the resulting struggle is not simply centered on the effort to maintain the legitimacy of a traditional moral system in the face of adverse structural processes. The complaint is principally directed toward a social and political entity; broadly defined, the struggle is a political contest. Though not understood by most Evangelicals in these terms, the political campaign Evangelicals wage is, in the main, aimed at a specific sector of American society recently labeled "the New Class."

The New Class

While there is no unanimity on what precisely the New Class is (P. Berger, 1978a; Bruce-Briggs, 1979; Gouldner, 1978; Horowitz, 1979), most who employ the term regard the New Class as the most recent historical variation of the general social phenomenon *class*—a social group distinguished by its special relationship to the means of production. Thus most accountable for changes in the class structure of any society (the disappearance of some classes and the emergence of new classes) are the changes that occur in the society's mechanism of production. In this case the changes responsible for the emergence of the New Class are those that have brought about what is variously known as postindustrial society or advanced industrial society. The New Class therefore is a fundamental structural fixture of all highly modern societies, not simply "late-capitalistic" ones. The most important social and economic characteristic of advanced industrial societies is an enormous new "knowledge industry"—an economic apparatus that provides the infrastructure for, among other things, the recent proliferation of the larger science-based industries (electronics, computers, etc.), the information industry (the media of mass communications, most importantly), and the public sector of government (public policy and research) (Machlup, 1962). The New Class, then, most generally consists of those college and professionally trained people who are occupationally associated with this knowledge industry. Put differently, the New Class comprises those who derive their livelihoods from the creation and manipulation of symbols. What is unique is not the occupational categories, for though some are new, others have existed for a long time. It is the quantitative shift in the number of those who fill these roles. Since World War II the percentage of those in the labor force performing these kinds of services has increased dramatically relative to those involved in producing material goods.

Because of the broad occupational diversity that exists within this class, one would expect to find some diversity of world view. While this is true, the New Class, like all social classes, approaches consensus on certain central perceptions. Underlying any diversity in New-Class world view is a more deeply rooted and commonly shared secular humanism. The basis for it is the marked tendency toward rationalistic modes of thought and discourse unmatched by any social grouping its size in history. The functions the New Class performs structurally necessitate this rationalism, which, moreover, fosters what has been termed "the culture of critical discourse" (Gouldner, 1978). The culture of critical discourse is a historically evolved set of rules concerning the nature and direction of social discourse. Those imbued with this orientation tend always to justify and legitimate perceptions, assertions, and courses of action solely on the basis of rationally deduced arguments and not on the basis of traditional societal authority—religious, bureaucratic, or familial. Normative patterns of thought, behavior, and lifestyle grounded in traditional (and often "irrational") sources of authority are therefore delegitimated as a matter of course. The culture of critical discourse thus defines as normative a high level of disenchantment, or secularity, in a world view. This does not mean that all members of the New Class are nonreligious, for clearly many are religious. Most concede to the ascendancy of modern rationalism, however, and insist that religious belief and moral conviction are plausible and justifiable only if they stand up to the rigor of logic and reason. In this form of rationalism the constituents of the New Class find a cohesive cognitive and linguistic base that transcends internal social, political, and occupational differentiation.

The humanistic dimension in the New-Class world view is derived from a long-standing liberal tradition in Western history. Humanism is ostensibly open, cosmopolitan, and tolerant. Most significantly, however, it claims a moral orientation toward, compassion for, and identification with the victims of social injustice and inequality and a conviction that man is the measure of all things. New-Class humanism is, in this sense, a morality of possibility. It is typically expressed in the tendency of New-Class members to measure existing social conditions against abstract and normative standards —against an ideal conception of what life could or should be. Social, political, and economic institutions are expected to embody these ideals. The concrete consequence is a commonly shared sense of calling (in varying intensities) to "serve the best interests of mankind." In the United States this calling is most widely expressed as "public interest."

A highly rational mode of thought and discourse in conjunction with a liberal cosmopolitanism and humanistic moralism thus provide the structure of New-Class ideology, but there is more. To speak of the New Class as a class is to suggest that it possesses a more or less collective body of political and economic interests. (Whether it perceives itself as a class with these interests is not at issue here.) The world view of the New Class suggests its political orientation. In the West, particularly in America, the social and political character of the New Class is predominantly, though not uniformly, left-liberal. This takes many forms: moderate hostility to monopoly capitalism, government interventionism in the private sector of the economy and the consequent expansion of public-sector services, the collectivization of private property, and a liberal-reformist orientation to social and political issues in general.

The New Class started to emerge as a sizable phenomenon only after World War II, but its social and political potential did not find sharp expression until the mid-1960s antiwar movement. Other New-Class political initiatives are behind the rise of public-interest organizations, consumer-protection groups, and governmental regulatory agencies most importantly, which are designed to educate and defend the ordinary citizen from the consequences of unharnessed business interests. Related involvements are the organized opposition to the development and proliferation of nuclear power and weaponry and the ecology movement, from local efforts to large-scale governmental efforts like the Environmental Protection Agency. New-Class social and political initiatives are also seen in the women's liberation movement, the gay rights movement, the civil rights movement, the antipoverty movement of the early 1960s, and the antismoking campaign.[2] Public interest is in this sense the New-Class vested interest—its source of economic and political power. In the private sphere, this humanistic moralism typically translates into moral tolerance, if not the actual propagation, of liberated lifestyles that include experimentation in courtship patterns, family structure, child rearing, and sexual life. The New Class is the vanguard in this type of moral revolution.

There are, however, dimensions of the New-Class world view that are decidedly antimodern; they spring typically from the New Class's humanistic inclinations. When factions of the New Class deride, for example, the "insanity of nuclear proliferation" and the "autonomy of techniques over human need in modern society," they reveal a distinct antimodern value orientation. This orientation is similarly expressed in the private-sphere quest of some New-Class members for "simplicity" and "natural living environments" and in the glorification of the "primordial self fully actualized"—inclinations largely incompatible with the modern technological and bureaucratic ethos. Moral ambiguity does exist within the New Class. Their dominant public-sphere values are, however, oriented toward technical mastery and professionalism and a commitment to the development of rationality in all its forms; likewise their predominant private-sphere values are oriented toward moral tolerance. Those New Class members who maintain the more antimodern perspective are in the minority, their values less salient. Thus in spite of diversity the rapprochement between the world view of the New Class and the world view of modernity is strong; the New Class can be considered the most modern class in history.

It is plain, then, how the New Class is located within the broader discussion. The net effect of the New Class's pursuit of its class interests has been the intensification of the erosion of traditional moral meanings in the larger culture. The deinstitutionalization of traditional moral definitions becomes, therefore, an unwitting part of the public agenda of the New Class.

Facing Up to the New Class

Evangelicals tacitly acknowledge the role of the New Class in aggravating the problem of moral decline. From the Evangelical perspective, the problem is grounded in an ideology: "Most of the evils in the world today can be traced to humanism . . . it is destroying our culture, families, country—and one day, the entire world" (LaHaye, 1980:9). According to LaHaye (1980: 130) the five doctrines of humanism are atheism, evolution, amorality (the rejection of absolute morals), the deification of man, and atheistic socialism. Put in different terms by another commentator:

> Humanism is the godless, groundless secular religion which underlies the warped and dangerous thinking behind much of the social activism of our time. It is satanic in origin. It represents man's effort to solve his problems and shape his society apart from God. It is exactly opposite of true Christianity, which seeks the guidance of the Word of God for the solution of human problems. (Rowe, 1976:43)

In contemporary American society, said Billings (1980b), "God has been kicked out, and humanism [has been] enthroned" (p. 3).

At the same time Evangelicals see the source of the perplexities in an amorphous category of people:

> In the last thirty years or so, the doctrines of liberals—and particularly their concept of the law—have become ever more embedded in the thinking of our opinion makers and legislators. . . . Every day, these demolition crews [are] at work, dynamiting the foundations of our liberties on the pretext of accomplishing some overriding social good. (Helms, 1976:26)

> But within my own lifetime, I have seen ferocious assaults on Christian faith and morals, first on the part of the intellectual community, and then on the part of the government. (Helms, 1976:15)

Some are more specific in identifying particular sources of particular problems, abortion, for example: "The major pressure for abortion has come from teenagers, unwed mothers, and career women, and from pregnant fashionable women who don't want the 'bother' of a baby" (Price, 1976:97). Contributing to this problem is the United States Supreme Court: "In the 1973 abortion decision the Court again tried to put itself in God's place. The Court decreed that life is a gift of the state" (Price, 1976:87). On homosexuality, it is not merely the homosexuals, but those whose "efforts in many states to 'de-criminalize' homosexuality only make the problem worse" (Price, 1976:72). Sexual license is encouraged partly by popular music "stars, who are willing to sing favorably of sin [adultery and sex] for money" (Price, 1976:82). Television network executives are also partly to blame for programming "inordinate amount[s] of violence" and "sexual content." The same indictment applies to the movie industry. Public educators are also to blame for encouraging sexual permissiveness by allowing "our schools to become smut factories, [and] our textbooks sex books" (Billings, 1980b:3). Also "we've forgotten our God-given responsibility to educate our children. Instead we have left it to the government, which has easily agreed and now takes the position that our children's education is their exclusive right" (Price, 1976:78).

On public issues, Evangelical opinion essentially corresponds to the broader conservative critique. Inflation is the result of government's many regulatory agencies, commissions, and bureaus. But according to Helms (1976), the problem does not stop there: "The most insidious assaults on our economy have occurred, not in the market place, but in the classroom of colleges and universities" (p. 30). Another author notes that "our college students, the leaders of America in years to come are being 'carefully taught' to be anti-business" (Price, 1976:77). Another assault on the economy comes from "environmentalists and consumerists [who have] declared open season on American business" (Helms, 1976:4). Contributing to the intensification of all of these problems are humanist organizations (the American Civil Liberties Union, the Americans for Democratic Action, the American Ethical Union, the Sex Information and Educational Council of the United States, and the National Organization of Women among many others), humanist educators (beginning with John Dewey), and the media (television, radio, newspapers, the movie industry, and magazines) (LaHaye, 1980:163). "America's TV networks and certain newspapers and magazines have gone out of their way to support the very people and the very doctrines which have brought the nation to its current crisis state" (Price, 1976:85).

By identifying intellectuals and the professoriat, career women, the courts, legislators, the television industry, public educators, government regulatory bureaucrats, and liberals in general as responsible for the perceived social and cultural decline in America, Evangelicals are, in fact, placing the blame on the New Class. One Evangelical commentator goes as far as to assert the conspiratorial notion that America's degeneracy has been through design: "[Humanists] are the mortal enemy of all pro-moral Americans, and the most serious threat to our nation in its entire history" (LaHaye, 1980: 187). Here the ideological and political challenge of Evangelicals to the New Class is most sharply articulated.

The "Young Evangelicals"

It is, of course, simplistic to view the contest between Evangelicalism and the New Class as a struggle between two distinct polarities given the diversity within both groups. One of the more interesting and unusual contradictions is found in a group that has been typed the "Young Evangelicals" —a group primarily made up of a younger generation of conservative Protestant clergy, intellectuals, professionals and semiprofessionals, seminarians, and journalists.

Given the definition of class used here, all of those involved in the production, distribution, manipulation and administration of religious symbols would also be members of the New Class. Mainstream Protestantism, especially its spokespeople, is very closely aligned with the political values and ideology of the larger, secular New Class. Among conservative Protestants one would expect there to be little if any sympathy with the New Class world view, yet there exists this minority that is, on almost all counts, aligned with the New Class (J. D. Hunter, 1980b). A thematic analysis of the articles in its two most important periodicals, *Sojourners* and *The Other Side*, revealed an almost complete and uncritical alliance with left-liberal political values and ideology: the advocacy of the liberal definition of human liberation and alternative lifestyles (although not sexual lifestyles); the left-liberal critique of big business, American "imperialistic" foreign policy, and the American military establishment; the presentation of the theological imperatives and justifications for social and political activism to promulgate their agenda. The most notable exception to their political and ideological rapprochement with the New Class is their antiabortion stance, although even on this point *Sojourners* showed considerable hesitancy, not going public against abortion until 1980.

The accommodation, even aculturation, of these conservative Protestants to the New Class is noteworthy, for the alignment is hardly coincidental. Their growth or decline is intricately tied to the well-being of the New Class as a whole. Indeed one might suspect that with time they will move to the left theologically in line with their move to the political left. Whether they are truly radical Christians capable of effecting political and social justice in the world or a politically innocuous group of Protestants riding the tide of political fashion, the Young Evangelicals are an interesting example of diversity in the conservative Protestant community. They also represent a potentially important source of disagreement within the larger Evangelical world.

Solutions to America's Moral Dilemma

While distressed by the decline of social, cultural (moral), and economic conditions in America, most Evangelicals believe that all is not lost, that a solution exists to the dilemma of modern America. Of the religious traditions in American history, conservative Protestantism has, more than all others, consistently maintained, if not explicitly then implicitly, the vision of an America in covenant with God, chosen by Him above all others for a special purpose. Contemporary Evangelicalism, by and large, retains this vision to the present: "The history of God's relationship with America is truly remarkable. Our Lord has intimately involved himself in our nation's history and thus has been instrumental in the establishment and growth of a free and vibrant country" (Price, 1976:184). America is still widely perceived as a nation founded on biblical values, beliefs, and morals: "God is just as involved in our nation's future as he has been in our past" (Price, 1976:184).

Thus, the deinstitutionalization of Christian morality is perceived as an assault on this covenant relationship. America as a nation is disobedient to God's will. Historically, this is not novel. Enlightenment rationalism and humanism were roundly perceived as disobedience to God and a threat to the covenant bond. President Lincoln in the nineteenth century articulated the fear of many when he claimed that the sin of slavery would not be without divine retribution. Fundamentalists in the early twentieth century believed America to be testing the patience of God with theological liberalism and the wide-scale use of alcohol. Finally, separatist Fundamentalists in the 1950s perceived an internally bred communism as a dangerous threat to the longevity of the American spirit and the covenant relationship. This perception has merely been revived in the present by a recognition of the institutional faltering of the traditional morality.

The consequences of continued disobedience are plain. As a father will punish his errant son, so will God punish America: "America has been richly blessed by God, and yet today we find ourselves in ever-increasing sin. God's chastisement, to turn us back to him, would appear from God's Word to be our present status" (Price, 1976:125). America is at a strategic point in its history, its greatest crisis, many Evangelicals maintain. Unless social conditions change back to morally acceptable limits, it is held, America will suffer the consequences of its disobedience. The broken covenant will result in America's social, cultural, political, and economic demise. America will come to the end of its history as a free and Christian nation.

The solution is clear: "America is sick today because we have a spiritual malady; we have forgotten our maker" (Noorbergen and Hood, 1980:185), or "America is in desperate need of divine healing; which can only come if God's people will humble themselves, pray, seek His face, and turn from their wicked ways" (Falwell, 1980b:243). Thus the duty of true believers is to call America to repentance. "Extensive changes in America will only come about after we experience national spiritual repentance, not before" (Price, 1976:229). While the spiritual factor in social change is considered preeminent, the solution does not stop there. There is the conviction that restoring America to its former state of moral propriety and therefore national resilience must be actively pursued.

TABLE 7.1

EVANGELICAL LITERATURE CONCERNED WITH LIFESTYLE BY PUBLISHER
(in percentages)

	Bethany	Gospel Light	Moody	Revell/Spire
Marriage/divorce	15.4	17.4	12.0	16.0
Family	46.1	43.5	60.0	40.0
Relationships	15.4	39.1	24.0	28.0
Miscellaneous	23.1	0.0	4.0	16.0
	100.0	100.0	100.0	100.0
N =	(26)	(23)	(25)	(25)

The solution thus entails not only spiritual but practical resistance to the erosion of morality. Perhaps the most important line of resistance is the local Evangelical congregation. The moral preachment and encouragement of Evangelical ministers typically reaffirms the ideological solidarity of local church members already disposed toward traditional stances. Content analysis of popular Evangelical literature (see Appendix 2) reveals another means of resistance. Of all popular Evangelical literature reviewed, 14.9 percent was devoted to lifestyle and morality concerns. Within this category, 18.4 percent dealt with the contemporary problems of courtship, marriage, and divorce; 43.5 percent confronted the dynamics of family living, child rearing, and particular private-sphere roles in the modern situation; 26.3 percent addressed the perplexities of individual morality, sexuality, and human relationships in general in the present context; and finally, 11.8 percent constituted a residual category of popular books dealing with home finance, Christian dieting, homemaking, and time-management and career-related topics (see Table 7.1). At the very least, this large body of literature indicates the concern Evangelicals have for these issues; practically, it goes a long way toward reaffirming traditional solutions to the ambiguities of life in modern social conditions.

Resistance to these modern processes finds its most daring and public expression in the form of conventional political activism. Providing direction and momentum for this drive are a small number of multimillion-dollar, national, Evangelical-based political organizations designed to encourage voter registration and voter turnout, to educate the electorate on the nature of current political issues, to persuade the electorate to support candidates who defend traditional values in domestic and foreign policy and oppose candidates who undermine them, and to lobby the American Congress on the legislation these Evangelical political organizations support. The most important of these are the Moral Majority (founded in 1979 by Falwell), Christian Voice, and the Religious Roundtable. All of these groups claim in so many words to be prolife, profamily, promoral, and pro-America. This is

Scripture	Tyndale	Word	Zondervan	Total
16.0	22.5	20.8	21.6	18.4
28.0	42.5	50.0	11.2	43.5
40.0	20.0	20.8	27.4	26.3
16.0	15.0	8.4	9.8	11.8
100.0	100.0	100.0	100.0	100.0
(25)	(40)	(24)	(51)	(239)

not to mention the numerous Evangelical single-issue organizations such as the Coalition for Better Television.

Popular Evangelical support for the public and political initiatives of these kinds of religious lobbies is suggested by Table 6.3, which concerns the relative importance of religious organizations making public statements on spiritual and religious matters, ethical and moral matters, and political and economic matters. The table clearly indicates the greater commitment of Evangelicals above all other religious groups in support of such action. The further breakdown of this data can be found in Table 7.2. Evangelical Protestants (92.0%) believe it is very important that religious organizations make public statements about spiritual and religious matters. Much lower percentages of liberal Protestants, Catholics, non-Christians, and secularists

TABLE 7.2

POLITICAL ACTIVISM BY RELIGIOUS PREFERENCE (in percentages)

	Evangelical	Liberal	Catholic	Non-Christian	Secularist
It is important for religious organizations to make public statements on:					
Spiritual and religious matters					
	92.0	76.4	80.2	43.4	45.9
Ethical and moral matters					
	88.1	69.2	77.8	37.7	43.4
Political and economic matters					
	58.4	40.4	48.0	34.0	27.5
Persuading elected officials: Religious organizations . . .					
Should	62.4	40.3	47.3	37.3	27.9
Should not	37.6	59.7	52.7	62.7	72.1
	100.0	100.0	100.0	100.0	100.0
N =	(347)	(540)	(474)	(56)	(132)

hold the same opinion. The breakdown follows a similar pattern in the other dimensions measured, but with lower percentages for all groups. On the importance of religious organizations making public statements on ethical and moral matters, Evangelicals lead with 88.1 percent; on political and economic issues, they lead with 58.4 percent. This perspective is even further supported by the data at the bottom of Table 7.2. On the propriety of religious organizations persuading senators and representatives to enact legislation they would like to see become law, 62.4 percent of all Evangelicals believe it is a good thing. Catholics, liberal Protestants, non-Christians, and secularists follow in descending order. These percentages are significant in light of the well-documented fact that conservative Protestants in the 1950s and 1960s maintained virtually the opposite opinion—that religion should remain quietist, oriented toward spiritual matters alone (Wuthnow, 1983). The more recent politization of Evangelicals attests to their recognition of the threat to traditional moral propriety and the importance they give to its continued hegemony in the culture.

Partly a result of the success of the efforts of the Evangelical political groups (at least as it is measured by the media attention they have received from their inception), Evangelicals as a population have increasingly come to perceive the importance of individual political responsibility. The Christian duty is to "elect God-centered men and women to the school boards, to the state legislature and the the U.S. Congress" (Walton, 1975:134). Voting is regarded as a provision of God. Another flyer published by the Religious Roundtable reiterates the importance of critical reflection and participation in the electoral process; concerning the vote, if "you vote prayerfully and responsibly, not according to party but according to principle, you will be doing your part to help select God-centered leaders" (Rowe, 1980:3). In addition to voting, Evangelicals are encouraged to:

> Work vigorously to expose amoral candidates and incumbents.
> Promote the national drive to register Christians.
> Join local, state, and national pro-moral organizations.
> Consider running for public office.
> Contribute to good, pro-moral causes. (LaHaye, 1980:225–237)[3]

The *Christian's Political Action Manual* (Billings, 1980a), which contains practical strategies for getting involved in a political campaign, affirms the viability of conventional political action to bring about social change.

Status Politics and the Politics of Resentment

The solution to moral perplexities posed by modernity and intensified by the New Class is, then, both spiritual (requiring repentance) and practical (involving well-organized political activism). Although resistance to modernity is the principal reason for the politization of large sectors of the Evangelical community, there is another, albeit less important, reason. The social-scientific literature that attempted to account for the radical right of the 1950s relied heavily on the notion of *status politics* (Bell, 1964; Gusfield, 1963; Lipset, 1963; Lipset and Raab, 1970). The status politics hypothesis basically asserted that populist political fervor in the United States occurred at that time as an effort to regain lost social prestige by those being left behind by history and social progress. Populist leaders of the 1950s advocated a return to a period in history in which their view of the world was dominant. Whether or not this hypothesis was true at that time, I contend that elements of it apply here, with an important difference. Rather than viewing populists and Evangelicals as a peculiar minority set against the rest of the world, the current situation can best be viewed as a relatively mainstream conservative Protestant community in competition with a cohort of knowledge elites and semielites—the New Class. Thus the status discrepancies between the elite and semielite New Class and mainstream Evangelicalism, which is predominantly middle and working class, are a source of friction between the two. Members of the New Class are quick to reveal their elitism by snubbing Evangelicals as "wild," "profoundly immature," "reactionary and dangerous" (J. D. Hunter, 1983). Evangelicals recognize the status ascendancy of the New Class—"[They have] taken over our government, the United Nations, education, television, and most of the other influential things of life" (LaHaye, 1980)—yet they see the New Class as dangerously corrupt and capable of subtle brainwashing.

Interestingly, each group perceives the other as totalitarian in impulse. From the New Class perspective, the "Protestant Right threatens pluralism, democracy and, yes, the American way. . . . These groups are on the march and are growing stronger each day. Their agenda is clear and frightening: they mean to capture the power of government and use it to establish a nightmare of religious and political orthodoxy" (American Civil Liberties Union, 1980). From the Evangelical perspective, "the humanist social planners present the greatest threat to human freedom and dignity in American history" (LaHaye, 1980). Most important to my argument is the tacit, if not conscious, awareness of Evangelicals that they have been replaced as the dominant political, social, and cultural force in American society, which necessarily contributes to their discontent. Nonetheless, the principal interest of Evangelicals then is not to regain social status but to push back the swelling tides of moral deinstitutionalization with which the New Class is associated. Success of the former interest may, however, be an important by-product of the success of the latter.[4]

Conclusions

The politization of large sectors of the Evangelical population during the late 1970s and early 1980s is from all indications real and not of little significance. At the same time, this conclusion does not support the perception, indeed contention, of many Evangelical leaders that they and their proposals have acquired mass support—that there is, in fact, a moral majority—and that there is ideological consensus among Evangelicals.

One analysis of national survey data concludes that, for the central proposals (on abortion, homosexuality, prayer and Bible reading in public schools, and women taking care of the home and family) that constitute the platform of the Moral Majority, there is, at the very most, 30 percent popular support nationwide (Simpson, 1983). Even in the Bible Belt, where one might suppose that there would be the strongest support for this organization and its agenda, there is no majority, no consensus (Shupe and Stacey, 1983).

Diversity is seen at other levels. Despite the rather republican view of political reality found in the utterances and literature of many Evangelical leaders, the survey data reveal that a Republican party preference is a minority choice within Evangelicalism, stronger only among the more highly educated, highly paid Evangelicals. When considering political self-identification, Evangelicals tend to identify themselves as right-of-center. There are significant numbers of Evangelicals, however, who identify themselves as politically neutral or politically left-of-center.[5] In the Reformed tradition, elements of a political liberalism are plainly noticeable. In the Anabaptist tradition, elements of a political left may be found. Black Evangelicals, many of whom belong to the Holiness-Pentecostal tradition, hold political values that are far from conservative Republican. Thus even though Evangelicals are clearly distressed about the shift in moral climate in American society and view political activism as a viable means of addressing this issue, they are not all unified behind one political course of action.

The significance of Evangelical political activism, however, lies not so much in the degree of ideological consensus, the amount of power Evangelicals possess in the American electorate, or the influence they may wield over elected political officials. Rather, it lies in the substance of their complaint in conjunction with the fact that this kind of activism exists at all in this social and historical context of broad-based resistance to modernity. Modernity creates conditions in which "immorality," from the Evangelical perspective, is structurally engendered. Bluntly put, modernity fosters "sin" in the culture, jeopardizing the moral covenant widely believed to exist between God and America. Understood in this context, the conflict is predictable. By resisting the sins engendered by modernity, Evangelicals resist modernity itself.[6]

The principal dimension of this resistance, however, is a political contest with the New Class—an elite class of workers in the knowledge industries. In the natural pursuit of their own social, economic, and political interests, the New Class intensifies the erosion process. Evangelicalism's political prowess (as exemplified by the formation and activism of groups like the Moral Majority and Christian Voice) implies the recognition that morality has become a political problem the solution to which is to be decided in the arena of competing interests and values. The friction between the New Class and the politicized factions of the Evangelical movement is only heightened by the discrepancies in prestige between the two groups; yet these discrepancies are secondary to those of interest and ideology. The interests at play are representative of world views distinguished by their differing relation to modernity: a world view that resists many of the constraints of modernity versus one that embodies to an unprecedented degree the perspectives and values of the modern world.

8

Legitimation: The Problem of Projection

All religions provide legitimations to one degree or another for the particular society in which they are embedded. Yet given the particular history of defiance in conservative Protestantism in modern America, it would be a historical irony to find religious legitimations of modernity in the world view of contemporary American Evangelicalism. It would also be reasonable to suggest, however, that Evangelicalism, to the degree that it is shaped by its interchange with modernity, would indeed tacitly legitimate the latter.

Legitimations are simply the explanations or justifications of a certain phenomenon. Religious legitimations are particularly important for they seek to explain phenomena by situating them within a cosmic and even supernatural frame of reference. As such, the problem of how religions legitimate social worlds is an extremely complex theoretical and empirical problem beyond the scope of this analysis; the pursuit of the issue of legitimation in the context of this work is thus limited. Rather than examine direct attempts to legitimate modernity by Evangelicals, my focus is on the way the Evangelical conception of God reflects the structural and cultural dimensions of modernity. If the nature of the Evangelical God embodies the character of modernity, then that may provide the ultimate religious legitimation inasmuch as the nature and purpose of God provides the very core of the Evangelical conception of absolute truth.

Explaining the nature of the gods is, from the perspective of the social sciences, the problem of projection. What all social-scientific theories on the origin of religion have in common is that they reduce the supernatural, and in particular the nature of God, to natural or material categories. They assume God to be a symbolic projection of some aspect of human experience (Grafton, 1941). What that aspect is, is a matter of debate. For Feuerbach (1957), the essence of religion, and the nature of God in particular, was anthropology: human nature purified, freed from the limits of individual man, made objective. For Freud (1953), it was the psychological as it related to harsh ecological conditions: a recapitulation of the infantile. God is merely the father figure elevated to a supernatural exponent. For Marx, it was ideological: God as a compensatory projection for those needs denied under capitalism. For Durkheim (1965), it was sociological: God is the hypostatization of society. Of other recent theories those of P. Berger (1969) and Falding (1977) are most notable. Underlying them all is the naturalistic presupposition that the gods are, at least in part, a human construction. Consonant with this idea is Schweitzer's (1948) observation that each epoch has found its reflection in Jesus; each epoch has sought to present Jesus in a form intelligible to its own time. If this is so, it is important to explore the ways in which contemporary American Evangelicals project the conditions of their existence onto their conception of God.[1]

In Christian theology, a most central feature of God's nature is a duality. God, as a spiritual being, is at once transcendent and imminent. The transcendent nature of God is marked by such qualities as omnipotence, omniscience, and omnipresence. God is self-existent, immutable, and eternal, transcending the limitations of time and space (history and culture). His divine person and will are absolutely and eternally holy, righteous, and true. Yet God is not always distant, detached from everyday life. He is present and knowable. The imminent nature of God is marked by such qualities as magnanimity and infinite love and good will for his creation, known principally through his redemptive plan, which culminates with the incarnation of God in Jesus Christ. It is also known by the sustaining and persevering presence and power of the Holy Spirit. This theological duality has bearing on the present discussion because it parallels the modern structural duality of the public and the private. The instrumentalism of God's transcendent nature parallels the instrumentalism of the public sphere of modern life. The expressivism of his imminent nature parallels the expressivism of the private sphere.

One could argue that this has always been the case and that if such a parallel exists, it is simply a result of happenstance. Yet what gives credence to this initially abstruse line of reasoning is the particular manner in which the theological duality is interpreted by modern Evangelicals. They understand God's transcendent and imminent nature largely in terms that parallel the subtleties of contemporary life experience in the public and private spheres. Clarity on this point is essential. I am not arguing that God's duality is in itself a projection of the public–private dichotomy. Obviously, this duality has existed in Jewish and Christian theologies from their inception, long before a public–private split emerged. Rather, I argue only that the manner in which divine transcendence and divine imminence is presently understood by Evangelicals is largely a result of their projection of the nature of the public–private spheres onto this theological duality. The duality as such latently and conveniently serves to legitimate people's experience of the public–private split in modern society.

The dual nature of God has traditionally been translated in the popular imagination in a particular way. Throughout Western history, God has presented two faces. In the Puritan conception of God (a conception which may be taken as typical), transcendence was understood in terms of the wrath, the terror, and the awesomeness of an infinitely powerful and "untamable" God. One might mention Jonathan Edwards's portrayal of the providence of an "angry God," Joseph Bellamy's notion of the "vindictive justice of the divine nature," and the general Puritan conviction of God's absolute sovereignty and justice with respect to salvation and damnation. Imminence, on the other hand, was understood mostly in terms of the kindness and mercy of the benevolent sovereign, God as a present source of help in time of need.

Of the two faces of God, the face of divine sovereignty and impartial justice has been preeminent. The love of God, for example, has always been understood in relation to his justice, rarely independent of it. The transcendent side of God retained a preeminence even in the pietistic movements in the West, which typically emphasized the love and grace of God toward men and his immediate availability to humankind through prayer, worship, and meditation. Such a conception of God proceeded upon a more fundamental recognition of God's transcendent moral perfection and holiness. Put differently, God has never been understood in casual or informal terms. Opposing what could have been called a presumptuous familiarity, John Wesley, whose pietistic leanings are well known, wrote:

> A Christian cannot think of the Author of his being without abasing himself before him, without a deep sense of the distance between a worm of earth and him that "sitteth on the circle of the heavens." In his presence he sinks into the dust, knowing himself to be less than nothing in his eye and being conscious, in a manner words cannot express, of his own littleness, ignorance, foolishness. (Outler, 1964)

A fearful awareness of this spiritual distance, it was believed, preceded any spiritual intimacy or mystical union between the Creator and his created. In this sense, the instrumentalism of God has historically preceded his expressivism. Transcendence, in the popular imagination, has loomed above imminence.

The situation is altogether different in contemporary Evangelicalism. To begin with, transcendence as a characteristic of God's nature has lost its predominance in the imagery of God in conservative Protestantism. When it is referred to, it is in very untraditional terms. Transcendence has been largely reinterpreted. *Sovereignty* has been translated to mean rational authority. *Providential direction of the church* has been redefined to mean the efficient administration of spiritual affairs in the world. *Divine anger, wrath,* and *vengeance,* if not eliminated entirely from Evangelical imagery, have been redefined to mean divine disappointment, regret, and grudgingness. Common enough is the use of the administrative metaphor to refer to God:

> God is in the business of saving souls.
> God owns my business and God owns me. I have every confidence He will take care of His property! (Tam, 1969:155)
> When the Lord has a job for you to do, He'll give you the strength and ability to do it. (Tam, 1969:206)
> The business of the Lord Jesus Christ is to represent you.
> Make an appointment with God for a quiet time. (R. Foster, n.d.)

All of these examples suggest the imagery of one who has rationalized the organization and administration of spiritual affairs. In the extreme, one even finds the practice of appointing Jesus Christ "chairman of the board" or "senior Partner" of companies owned by Evangelicals.[2] In caricature, the image of God has changed from the capricious and mighty sovereign to that of the benign bureaucrat.

What is most significant, however, in this shift in anthropomorphic imagery is not the facile likening of God to bureaucrats, businessmen, and so on; rather, it is the deemphasis of God's transcent nature occasioned by the emphasis of his imminent nature. The image of God as Lord of Lords, King of Kings, Creator of heaven and earth, although still an important part of the Evangelical world view, has become a nominal and thus less stirring image as a result of the increasing value put on God's imminent and expressive nature: "Wrongly do we think of God as rigid, impassive, sad and stern. . . . He is the Source of all genuine joy" (Flynn, 1980:21).

In different terms, Freudians and non-Freudians alike have noted the paternal and maternal expressions of divinity. The paternal nature of God (God the Father) is understood as strong, hard, stern, wrathful, all-wise, firm, and so on. The maternal nature of God is understood in terms of attributes such as warmth, kindness, helpfulness, love, gentleness, and patience. The conceptual parallel between paternalism–maternalism and instrumentalism–expressivity as constructs for describing the transcendent and imminent nature of God is obvious. In these alternate terms, the maternal attributes of God have acquired unprecedented importance in the image of God. Indeed, recent empirical research comparing Catholics to Evangelicals documents this assertion (Keyser and Collins, 1976; cf. Chartier and Goehner, 1976). Compared to Catholics, Evangelicals perceived God as more maternal. Though God is still addressed as "Father," among Evangelicals he is viewed as equally paternal and maternal in his divine attributes.

Thus while the imminent (expressive or maternal) nature of God has gained importance in the Evangelical perspective, imminence has undergone a reinterpretation of its own. God's love is understood to mean more than the grace and mercy shown in salvation. It has acquired in addition two more salient, inner-worldly dimensions. These dimensions are not to be confused with the Puritan notion of godly benevolence: divine favor in a person's life circumstances yielding an increased measure of health and prosperity. On the one hand, love has, in many respects, come to mean divine tolerance: God loves one just as one is, and this is so even if one rejects him. In the world, God's posture toward the heretic and the infidel is one of patience and leniency. God does punish and chastise, but never in anger. "We should learn to stop reacting as if God is an angry, irrational, and unpredictable Parent who is just waiting for us to get out of line so He can belt us" (T. Foster, 1980:70). On the other hand, this love of God is subjectivistic. It is revealed in God's infinite capacity to care for man's emotional and psychological problems. In one monograph Christian psychologist T. Foster (1980) has explored the "Abba," or what Foster calls the "Daddy" aspect, of God's "personality" in relation to emotional and mental health:

> Remember what it was like to be a young child? Imagine yourself sitting on your daddy's lap. There is a loud thunderstorm outside, but you are safe because you are with your daddy. If its been a while since you felt that same warm, secure feeling with God, both you and Abba will enjoy a closer, warmer, more dependent relationship that comes when there is no power struggle. Abba delights in your trusting Him. (p. 62)

> Abba is waiting for you to come to Him with your messes and your hurts and to depend on Him. Tell Him all about your problems and ask Him for His help. He hears and He cares. (p. 96)

Slogans announce that "Jesus is the bridge over troubled water," that "God understands our every need," that "Christ is Himself a Friend to lean upon in times of trouble," and that "God is the Great Counselor."

It is not enough to note that God has been ascribed psychiatric capabilities. Of equal significance is the fact that he is regarded in such familiar and informal terms. He is frequently referred to as our "Friend," our "Companion," our "Helper," and sometimes as our "Co-pilot." We are told that one may "discover a new intimacy with [our] Heavenly Father" (T. Foster, 1980:jacket). The soteriological requirement of a "personal relationship" with God—that a personal and intimate relationship with God is even possible—also underlines this informality. The sense of social and spiritual distance that formerly existed between God and his church has thus been sharply reduced. The imagery of the imminence of God has translated from Divine Protector to Best Friend.

In this manner the image of God in conservative Protestantism has come to acquire some of the characteristics of modernity. The transcendent nature of God reflects the functional rationality dominant in the public sphere. Efficiency, rationality, practicality, and sensibility are all attributes of the divine character. The imminent nature of God reflects the consequences of cultural pluralism and structural pluralism. His image reflects a measure of tolerance toward nonbelievers. It also reflects the subjectivism that pervades the private sphere. Moreover, the image of God reflects the contemporaneity of democratic informality. The incarnation has come to mean, among other things, that God has become one of us; therefore he may be regarded and treated as one of us. The ascendancy of the imminent nature of God over his transcendent nature may be understood partly in terms of the pietistic orientation of contemporary Evangelicalism in contrast to the asceticism of early American Puritanism—that is, the current ascendancy in conservative Protestantism of the Baptist and Holiness-Pentecostal traditions over the Reformational traditions dominant earlier in American conservative Protestant history. It must also be understood as reflecting the accommodation to the pressures of privatization. God's nature reflects the relative insignificance and inefficacy of conservative Protestant symbols in the public sphere of modern life. Conversely, it reflects the widening relevance of the Evangelical world view to the private sphere.

There is diversity in the Evangelical subculture on this issue as on the others I have presented. Among the Reformational-Confessional denominations and Anabaptist denominations, themes of sovereignty are in greater evidence. Overall, however, the foregoing picture applies. Whatever else may be said, the fire, the caprice, and the majesty that formerly pervaded the imagery of God is largely gone. The vision of a God whose "thoughts are not our thoughts" and whose "ways are not our ways" has all but vanished. Such a perception lacks plausibility in the modern situation. Instead and more consonant with the modern scene, God has become predictably rational, tolerant, familiar, and subjectivistic. Insofar as the image of God has become redefined in this way, God has become domesticated in the consciousness of Evangelicals. His image is less capable of stirring the thoughts and emotions. In this manner as well, the imagery of the contemporary Evangelical God provides a tacit though admittedly partial legitimation of the structural forces and cultural consequences of modernity.

There is one exception to this legitimating tendency: God is not always viewed as passive and pliable. In the affairs of individual spirituality and personal relationships, this vision is predominant; but with ambiguous social trends and questionable national affairs, God is not nearly so benign: "If we [as a nation] fail to turn to God, he will allow chastening to continue until we ultimately turn to him" (Price, 1976:11). By invoking the image of a God who is impatient with the disobedience of a nation; who is capable of chastising America for its sins with natural, social, economic, and military disasters; who will punish America for threatening to sever the covenant bond by its immorality—Evangelicals project an image of God that serves to delegitimate modernity. Implicit in God's repudiation of the sins of modernity is a partial repudiation of modernity itself. The transcendent nature of God, the vision of God as Judge, in this situation is reaffirmed. This vision sharply limits the legitimacy of the structural forces and cultural consequences of modernity in the Evangelical mind.

Overall, however, the image of God as the Judge of nations and of peoples constitutes a relatively small part of the Evangelical god concept. To the degree that the deinstitutionalization of morality as a sociocultural trend in America becomes associated with the breaking of the covenant between God and America, will this dimension of God's character be likely to increase in salience. Yet for the most part, the affairs of private life are of much greater, more immediate import to the Evangelical, so the "soft" side of God continues to dominate his image in the Evangelical world view.

Thus in the interchange that occurs between modernity and the world view of American Evangelicalism, the cycle is completed. There is accommodation to modernity; there is also very real and formidable resistance to dimensions of these historical processes. There is, accordingly, symbolic legitimation and delegitimation as well.

Part Four

CONCLUSIONS

9

The Ambivalence of Orthodoxy
in Contemporary America

Determining the proper place of religion in modern society is a problem that has perplexed, and promises to continue to perplex, theology, ecclesiology, and public policy alike. Yet, the de facto place of religion may or may not be related to the musings in those fields. This problem can only find resolution in the everyday lives of millions of ordinary people who continue to maintain a conviction about some form of religious truth. The types of solutions are literally as diverse as the myriad religions and the various expressions modernity takes in a society. No unidirectional hypothesis could adequately account for this range of empirical possibility. Nonetheless the systematic effort to understand the encounter between religion and modernity is an important undertaking in itself, not solely for the sake of expanding the range of human knowledge, but for the implications it may have for theology, ecclesiology, and public policy.

This book is one such attempt to understand the dynamics of the encounter between modernity and a particular religious world view, American Evangelicalism, not as perceived by the theologian, but as experienced by the man on the street. Yet because of Evangelicalism's own inner diversity, simple summarization is confounded. Although American Evangelicalism is not monolithic either as a sociocultural phenomenon or (partly as a result of the former) in its response to the perplexities of modernity, it is, nevertheless, possible to speak of a mainstream or dominant impulse. My attempt throughout has been to focus on the mainstream while accounting for diversity.

The social transformations that occurred within American society in the past century owing to the augmentation of the modernizing forces have been astonishing. The consequences of these changes for Evangelicalism have been equally traumatic. Overall, conservative Protestantism has gone from a position of cultural dominance and institutional power to varying levels of cultural subordination and social-structural insignificance. While many social scientists are professionally satisfied (and personally relieved) to leave the issue at that, the phenomenon cannot so easily be dismissed. Evangelicalism has as a result of its encounter with these modernizing forces undergone its own inner transformation.

As a background against which to understand this bargaining, one may turn to the demographic analysis. Demographically, Evangelicals as a whole are located furthest from key structural pressures of modernity: high levels of education, high mobility-inducing income levels, urbanization, and the public sphere of work. The relative isolation of Evangelicalism from these factors mitigates the threat of the world-disaffirming qualities of modernity. Orthodox beliefs and more demanding religious practices are much more easily sustained in this situation.

Thus, in response to the question Why has Evangelicalism not disappeared with the advent of modernity? a partial explanation would be that modernity is irregularly distributed in society. Contemporary Evangelicalism thrives in those sectors in which the forces of modernity are not strong. Another reason (one favored by Evangelicals) is that there are extraempirical (spiritual or supernatural) causes of Evangelicalism's sustained vitality: "It is not God's will for the truth to disappear; therefore God, in spite of all odds against him, protects the truth in the hearts and minds of his children." While social science cannot comment upon the verity or lack of verity of this possibility, it must at least acknowledge the possibility of this explanation.

Inasmuch as Evangelicalism is not totally insulated from the dominant society, a third partial explanation is that, in its encounter with modernity, Evangelicalism has made certain concessions by accommodating to some of the pressures that modernity imposes. These compromises thereby allow for an easing of the cognitive tensions. To the pressures of functional rationality, the specifically religious and spiritual dimensions of Evangelical experience are not translated into naturalistic rationalizations but are intensely methodized and systematized. To the pressures of cultural pluralism, Evangelical belief avoids the abandonment of its exclusiveness by becoming tempered and civilized. To the pressures of structural pluralism and privatization, Evangelical faith becomes embroiled in the modern phenomenon of intrasubjectivity to the point of approximating a hedonism and narcissism. In this, it avoids the "embarrassment" of appearing out of date and out of fashion. Thus, while Evangelicalism has been able to maintain its orthodoxy, its cultural style is very different from that which characterized it in prior centuries.

Though conciliatory at some levels, Evangelicals remain brashly resistant to modernity at others. Apart from a central theism, which it has yet to abandon, it is presently resistant to the loss of hegemony by what it sees as the traditional Christian morality dominant in American society. The threat is largely from the inevitable modern processes of wide-scale deinstitutionalization. The threat also emerges from the natural pursuit of collective interests on the part of the modern New Class. The issue has had the effect of politicizing large sections of the Evangelical community. As such, this has become a struggle which the greater number of Evangelicals have no intention of losing.

If this is the general resolution to the problem of modernity that this particular form of religious orthodoxy has found, what difference does it make? What are the implications for the longevity of Evangelicalism, for orthodoxy in general, and for modernity itself?

The Future of Evangelicalism, Orthodoxy, and Modernity

The data presented here provide general empirical verification for the notion that modernity is inimical to traditional religious belief. The very least one may say is that modernity does not provide an agreeable circumstance for religious belief to flourish. But modernity is more than this. Its symbols and its structure are deeply contrary to religious, supernaturalistic presuppositions. Religious world views, especially orthodoxies, are on the defensive, constrained to adjust to, account for, and deal with the world disaffirming sociocultural environment that modernity engenders. In this situation, religion will typically either seek to preserve its religious heritage by retreating (demographically and otherwise) from the encounter with modernity or in the encounter, compromise, bargaining creed for presumed longevity (e.g., the short-lived popularity of liberal Protestant theological innovations in the 1960s exemplifies this well). Evangelicalism has done a little of both.

What does this mean for the future of Evangelicalism and the Evangelical world view? Demographics plays an important role. The greatest popular support of Evangelicalism comes from the rural and small-town areas of the South and Midwest—the Bible Belt. The current national shift of industry and population to the South will invariably bring about the urbanization and industrialization, ipso facto the modernization, of these areas. The consequences of this shift for this bastion of conservative Protestantism are debatable. Evangelical values and perspectives are institutionalized deeply enough in this sociogeographic region that the short-term effects will probably be minimal. In fact, one may even find, for a time, the symbiotic growth of each: Evangelical ethical values providing a favorable cultural context for individual and corporate productivity; industry financially supporting the causes and concerns of the Evangelical community. Yet the congeniality of this relationship may be short-lived. The precedent for the long-term encounter of conservative Protestantism with modernization is established. Given the dominance of the modern world view in the culture as a whole, the long-term consequences are generally (not specifically) predictable. Presuming no cataclysmic changes in world affairs, the popular support in these areas will probably diminish.

Cognitive survival in this climate will require the continued effort to build and sustain a sociocultural world in which the Evangelical view of reality is actively supported, even taken for granted. Stable institutions acting as plausibility structures would be capable of reimposing their objectified meanings on a laity perplexed by the contrary realities of day-to-day life, of reassuring the doubter that things are all right after all. Evangelicalism has been successful thus far. Likely to pose problems in the future, however, is education, particularly at the higher levels. The growth of the Evangelical liberal arts movement in the past twenty-five years has been remarkable. Interestingly, it has become of major importance in the Evangelical community for Christian colleges to gain public (i.e., secular) recognition for the high-quality scholarship of their faculties in all disciplines. Yet any institution genuinely committed to scholarship and the spawning of serious critical Christian thought and discourse among its faculty and student body will have to realize the well-established fact that education, even Christian education, secularizes. Although a Christian college community may provide a safer context in which to become aware of alternative patterns of life and belief, any habits of philosophical reflection and independent and critical thinking a student acquires in college or university training are likely to remain with him. Increased levels of tolerance, for example, have been clearly related to greater educational achievement. Even more threatening, the chances for religious defection at the social-psychological level are greatly enhanced. Inasmuch as the future leadership of Evangelicalism is being groomed in these quarters, education may prove to be counterproductive for the survival of Protestant orthodoxy in America in the long run.

The future of Evangelicalism must be considered from a different though related angle as well. What further compromises will result from the sustained encounter with modernity? This, of course, is difficult to assess. Doctrinal innovations (such as the growing popularity of Barthian neoorthodoxy in some Evangelical seminaries, Fuller most notably) generated by an educated elite may at some point foster a theological backlash that could result in another divisive split in conservative Protestantism (between "reactionary" and "heretical" forces, depending on one's point of view). Although the greatest percentage of Evangelicals still maintain traditional doctrinal and moral positions, there is sufficient diversity in the general Evangelical population to perhaps imply a growing popular demand for the theological legitimations of doctrinal innovations. On the issue of inerrancy, the rumblings have already begun to sound.

At the same time, the policies of spiritual rationality, religious civility, and spiritual intrasubjectivity will probably continue unchanged for a long while. It seems unlikely, contrary to the opinion of some, that Evangelicalism will provide a collective ideology for a future of economic scarcity and social misery.[1] A Third Great Awakening, or a Second Protestant Reformation as it has been called, with the same amount of influence as the First and Second Great Awakenings in America, or as the original Protestant Reformation, is a virtual sociological, not to mention legal, impossibility under the present conditions of modernity. The social and economic conditions would have to change drastically for the worse for such a wide-scale revival to be even possible, and under these conditions, sweeping revival would still be unlikely. The example of the state of religious affairs during the Depression years is instructive on this point. The traditions of secularism have become too deeply engrained in American culture and institutional structure to permit anything but, at best, a large-scale, private-sphere renewal.

The future strength of the Evangelical movement and the purity of the Evangelical world view are, then, dubious. Popular support will undoubtedly lessen in the long run. It is also reasonable to predict that the Evangelical world view will undergo still further mutations that will make it even less similar to the historical faith than it already is—to the delight of some and the chagrin of others. Such mutations will undoubtedly be challenged. What do other orthodoxies that are soon to encounter, or are already encountering, these circumstances have to learn from the example of Evangelicalism? The theological and historical uniqueness of American Evangelicalism makes comparisons with other orthodoxies difficult, but general comments are possible.

As the form of religious orthodoxy to sustain the encounter with modernity longer and more intensely than any other, Evangelicalism reveals that, without total withdrawal, cognitive bargaining is unavoidable. On the American scene, conservative Catholicism and Orthodox Judaism have already begun to encounter the same problems. In the Catholic church the constraints of modernity have already stirred a great deal of theological unrest among theologians and moral unrest among sectors of the laity. Vatican II formally initiated the bargaining phase. Lay discontent with church policy on such matters as birth control, divorce, and priestly celibacy may ultimately force the ecclesiastical hierarchy into further ex cathedra compromises. Yet the affinities the Evangelical world view has historically had with modernity are not shared by Catholicism. This crucial difference will be important to the outcome; so too will differences in church stucture and authority (i.e., centralization versus decentralization). Conservative Catholicism may be better able to withstand the compromising situation.

Orthodox Judaism has had to face similar circumstances. Of Orthodox Judaism Heilman (1978) has written: "It recognizes the legitimacy of modernity insofar as it does not destroy Orthodoxy" (p. 33). Notwithstanding, modernity provides a situation in which modern Orthodox Jews reconstruct an interpretation of the past in terms of the present and of the present in terms of the past. This allows an Orthodox Jewish man, for example, "to wear a yalmulke on his head while smoking pot" or work "as a physician in an ultramodern research hospital but take Friday evenings and Saturdays off to observe his Sabbath" (Heilman, 1978:33). The contradictions between the older Orthodoxy and the modern world view are too fundamental to permit mutual coexistence without these accommodations.

Though cognitive bargaining is virtually unavoidable, the case of Evangelicalism thus far reveals that the rudimentary beliefs constituting the orthodoxy do not have to be involved in the exchange. In different words, traditional beliefs, as long as they are firmly buttressed by a stable institutional matrix, can remain relatively protected from the world-disaffirming realities of modernity. There is, then, as much as one can tell, a future for orthodoxy in contemporary society. Yet for those concerned with doctrinal and religious purity, or with the expansion of the kingdom of God on earth, this future promises in the long term to be less than cheerful.

Last, there are the implications of this analysis for an understanding of modernity. I have argued that, within the more modernized societies, the forces of modernity gain autonomy and ultimately become the dominant influence in a relationship with religion. From the classical period in sociological thought until only recently, most sociologists assumed that the secularizing propensities of modernity would proceed unchecked, with the ultimate consequence of forcing the extinction of all religious expression. It is clear on the basis of research on the recent surges of religious vitality (from Eastern mysticism to Catholic Pentecostalism) that this assumption can no longer be maintained. My research underlines this alternative thesis. The structural and symbolic forces of modernity plainly wield a vast and imposing influence on religion and the religious world view, yet there are equally clear limits to this influence. Modernity itself creates certain circumstances that evoke the bold reassertion of religious meanings, which can be, and in most cases are, directly contrary to the nature of modernity. The emergence of the new religions in the 1970s supports this; so too does the Evangelical defense against the erosion of traditional morality on the contemporary scene. The secularizing tendencies of modernity are thus checked, if not reversed, for a time. This research implies, among other things, that, in spite of a dominant (though not necessarily teleological) trend of disenchantment and deinstitutionalization of traditional religious meanings, cycles of religious upsurge are possible and even predictable under the conditions of modernity.

More than just a protest against the anomic and alienating phenomena built into modernity, religious upsurge and often the mere intransigence of religion in these circumstances also represents the human effort to harness the unruly and unkind forces of modernity, to regain control over what often appears from the street and from the academy to be the ineluctable march toward technological determinism, and to reimpose human value and meaning on areas of human experience from which these have been subtracted. How effective these efforts are and will be is a matter of conjecture.

This research has been an attempt to explain and interpret the consequences of both the encounter of one religious tradition with modernity and the manner in which the tradition has attempted to cope. The attempt was predicated on the belief that the Evangelical experience can be generally instructive in probing the classical sociological query What is the nature of individual existence in modern society? Dimensions of the Evangelical experience may be generalizable to the experience of all modern men. Implied in this exercise was the attempt to take seriously the world as Evangelicals define it and experience it. Too often in the social sciences and in the broader liberal culture, the Evangelical is sneered at as an anachronism or rebuffed as a curiosity to be treated with detached interest but not really to be taken seriously. Such an attitude may, in the end, be misguided. If the day does come (as the Evangelical believes it will), when "the skies open and the Son of Man comes in the clouds of heaven with great power and glory to gather his elect from the four winds" (cf. Matthew 24:30–31), more than one skeptic may be caught muttering under his breath: "Well, I'll be damned!"

APPENDIXES
NOTES
BIBLIOGRAPHY
INDEX

APPENDIX ONE

Operationalizing Evangelicalism

In performing an analysis with Evangelicalism as the subject, perhaps the greatest problem is how to operationalize—that is, define—*Evangelical* in measurable terms. One part of the problem is that there is no agreement on a conceptual definition. Theologians such as Emile Bruner, Karl Barth, E. J. Carnell, and Carl Henry have all used the term in different ways. The few sociologists who have examined Evangelicalism do not help matters either. As Warner (1979) has pointed out, there are fairly clear evaluative biases against Evangelicalism that have translated empirically into a genuine lack of sensitivity to the subject under consideration. One rough-shod tendency of these sociologists is to lump all conservative Protestants under one label—Fundamentalist—without any regard for the diversity within the subculture.

The problem is further compounded in the attempt to operationalize *Evangelical* in terms of denominational affiliation, an attempt that has dominated the research of the phenomenon. Typically, liberals are "found" in some denominations (Episcopal, Congregational, United Presbyterian, etc.), "Fundamentalists" in others (Southern Baptist, Free-Will Methodist, Church of the Nazarene, Church of Christ, the variety of Pentecostal denominations, etc.). Survey data show both Evangelicals and liberals are broadly based in all denominations. What has long been needed is an approach to the phenomenon that takes into account the intended meanings of the subjects under analysis. To do this, one must examine, from the Evangelical perspective, the theological issues that discriminate Evangelicals from other religious groups, especially Protestant ones (see Hunter, 1982, for an elaboration of this argument).

To begin at the very foundation, Evangelicalism is, historically, a Protestant phenomenon. There is a small contingent of "Catholic Evangelicals"— professing Catholics who hold to the general Evangelical theological orientation. So too there is an even smaller group of "Evangelical Jews"—the so-

139

called Jews for Jesus, or "fulfilled Jews." Both groups must be regarded as
something other than true Evangelicals. An important reason for this in the
case of the Catholics is the long-standing anti-Romanism of American conservative Protestantism. Only since the 1960s have there been any signs of
tolerance toward Rome on the part of Evangelicals. A firm distrust of anything that hints of the Catholic cosmology, even if it has been "Protes-
tantized," remains virtually unshakable. Even when such affinities exist,
Evangelicals, though sometimes willing to engage in ecumenical interchange, nonetheless are usually unwilling to be united under a common
classification. Moreover, among such Catholics and such Jews the "conversion" is only partial; they undergo a transformation of soteriology while remaining steadfast on other elements of their own traditions. Typically, all
parties can only agree that there are Protestant Christians, Catholic Christians, and Jewish Christians (with the word *Christian* being defined in
Evangelical terms).

One may say more about Evangelicalism than simply that it is a Protestant phenomenon. Essential to being an Evangelical is the affirmation of
two core theological propositions: the inerrancy of Scripture and the divinity
of Christ. As I point out in Chapter 3, these have remained the two central doctrines by which conservative Protestants have sought to be distinguished. In the interview schedule, belief in the inerrancy of the Bible was
measured by Answer 3 to the following question:

> Which *one* of these statements comes *closest* to describing your feelings about
> the Bible?
> 1. The Bible is a collection of writings representing some of the religious phi-
>   losophies of ancient man.
> 2. The Bible is the Word of God but is sometimes mistaken in its statements
>   and teachings.
> 3. The Bible is the Word of God and is *not* mistaken in its statements and
>   teachings.
> 4. Don't know.

Belief in the divinity of Christ was measured by Answer 1 *or* Answer 3 to the
following question:

> Which *one* of these statements comes *closest* to describing your feelings about
> Jesus Christ?
> 1. Jesus Christ was a man, but was divine in the sense that God worked
>   through Him; He was the Son of God.
> 2. Jesus Christ is not God or the Son of God, but was a great religious
>   teacher.
> 3. Jesus Christ is both fully God and fully man.
> 4. Don't know.

In the operationalization of *Evangelical* in the survey data, these three
items were held constant. The fourth item is the affirmation of the corollary

belief that salvation is through Jesus Christ. In this research there were three ways in which the respondents could have affirmed this belief, thereby distinguishing between two slightly different orientations within Evangelicalism toward the question of salvation: the confessional and the conversional. To qualify for the confessional category the respondent had to choose Answer 4 to the following question:

> Which *one* of these statements comes *closest* to describing your feelings about life after death?
> 1. There is no life after death.
> 2. There is life after death but what a person does in this life has no bearing on it.
> 3. Heaven is a divine reward for those who earn it by their good life.
> 4. The only hope for Heaven is through personal faith in Jesus Christ.
> 5. Don't know.

Those in the conversional category had to select Answer 1 to all of the following four questions:

> Have you ever had a religious experience—that is, a particularly powerful religious insight or awakening—that changed the direction of your life, or not?
> 1. Yes.   2. No.
> Is this experience still important to you in your everyday life, or not?
> 1. Yes.   2. No.   3. No opinion.
> Did this experience involve Jesus Christ, or not?
> 1. Yes.   2. No.   3. Don't remember.
> Was this a *conversion* experience—an identifiable turning point that included asking Jesus Christ to be your personal savior, or not?
> 1. Yes.   2. No.   3. Don't remember.

Finally, there were those who qualified for both categories.

For the purposes of this research, then, an *Evangelical* is a Protestant who attests to the inerrancy of Scripture and the divinity of Christ and either (1) believes that Jesus Christ is the only hope for salvation or (2) has had a religious experience—that is, a particularly powerful religious insight or awakening that is still important in his everyday life, that involved a conversion to Jesus Christ as his personal savior or (3) both (1) and (2). The breakdown of the study sample is as follows:

	Number	Percentage of total population
1. Confessional	154	9.94
2. Conversional	20	1.29
3. Confessional / Conversional	174	11.23
Total	348	22.46

APPENDIX TWO

Methodological Strategies

Survey Data

A central feature of my research was a secondary quantitative analysis of public opinion data. These data were taken from a survey conducted by the Princeton Religious Research Center for the private use of the Evangelical periodical *Christianity Today* during the period from November 1978 through February 1979. The survey was based on a modified probability sample of a cross-section of adult Americans (18 and older). The sample of 1,553 cases was stratified by age, gender, region, and education so as to approximate the noninstitutionalized adult civilian population of the United States. (It should be noted parenthetically that this is an attitudinal survey and not a census survey. Extreme precision in reporting demographic factors is neither assumed nor guaranteed.) Personal interviewing was the data-collection technique.

TABLE A.1

EVANGELICAL LITERATURE BY PUBLISHER (in percentages)

	Bethany	Gospel Light	Moody	Revell/Spire
Lifestyle	14.4	17.6	7.6	13.4
Emotional/psychological	7.2	19.9	8.2	14.4
Spiritual	32.8	18.3	32.2	32.6
Testimony	12.8	6.1	7.6	24.1
Bible	2.8	18.3	7.6	4.3
Evangelism	4.4	3.0	7.3	2.1
Scholarship	5.0	1.5	6.9	1.1
Popular theology	20.6	15.3	22.6	8.0
	100.0	100.0	100.0	100.0
N =	(180)	(131)	(331)	(187)

Archival Data

An overriding objective of my research was to analyze the Evangelical world view at the level of the man on the street. Content analysis of popular Evangelical literature was an important means of doing this. One type of content analysis I used was a thematic analysis—the analysis of broad but distinct themes in archival data. In this case, my data were popular Evangelical monographs. My problem was the reliable translation of this theoretical objective into specific methods of research. An elaboration of my strategy and a summary table are provided here.

First, I selected the publishers and titles from the *East Coast Distributors Catalogue*, which lists all the currently available publications of forty-four publishers of Evangelical books (Bible and music divisions excluded). From this list I selected eight of the largest Evangelical publishing houses, size being determined by the total number of books currently published. My assumption is that size is an indication of general acceptance in the Evangelical subculture. From this sample I selected only books rated by their publishers as either "trade paperbacks" or "mass-market" books. Thus, all booklets, teachers' editions, complete sets, and clothbound books were excluded. Also excluded were trade paper and mass-market series collections, because I thought their size and uniform character would skew the sample distribution. I assumed thus that, by analyzing Evangelical books of this genre, I could discover the predominant beliefs and concerns in the Evangelical world view at this level.

It turned out that the eight largest publishers are most representative of what I have called the Baptist tradition of Evangelicalism. The other traditions do have publishing houses, but they are typically very small. Con-

Scripture	Tyndale	Word	Zondervan	Total
20.3	29.4	18.5	13.1	14.9
18.7	14.7	18.5	9.5	12.3
27.6	25.7	30.0	23.3	28.0
2.4	7.4	6.1	4.3	8.6
6.5	2.9	2.2	19.0	9.4
4.1	5.1	3.1	3.6	4.3
4.9	3.7	3.1	2.6	3.8
15.5	11.1	18.5	24.6	18.7
100.0	100.0	100.0	100.0	100.0
(123)	(136)	(130)	(390)	(1608)

cordia Publishing House (of the Lutheran Church-Missouri Synod) in the Reformational-Confessional tradition, for example, publishes mostly booklets of Bible stories and Bible study aids, very few new titles. The few mass-market and trade publications Concordia produces do deal with lifestyle topics, emotional and psychological problems, and traditional theodicy. Other small publishers in the other traditions exhibit like patterns. The enormous volume of literature produced by publishing houses in the Baptist tradition is indicative of, if not one reason for, the current dominance of this tradition in American Evangelicalism.

Having selected the books, my next step was to categorize each volume thematically according to its predominant substantive concern (see Table A.1). Excluded from the summary table are the 312 miscellaneous books, a category that included, for example, sermons and speeches, quizzes and games, strategies for youth-group leadership, Christian humor, handicrafts, study guides, children's stories, and fiction. I considered their stylistic quality and programmatic intent sufficiently different to make their comparison to the other books inappropriate.

Of final note, the content-analytic tables in the text proper (Tables 6.4 and 7.1) refer to this larger analysis. They constitute the further breakdown of some of the broad categories listed here.

Notes

Chapter 1

1. Brode's compilation (1969) is a very helpful summary of this research.
2. Concerning the typological distinction between premodern and modern societies and the typological tradition in modernization theory, see the excellent compendium in Tonnies, 1957:12–29; cf. Boulding, 1964; Polanyi, 1944.
3. For an elaboration of these criticisms, see Eisenstadt, 1973:101 ff.
4. One will immediately recognize my indebtedness to P. Berger, B. Berger, and Kellner for their suggestions in this section; see P. Berger et al., 1974:9.
5. This typology was, like Weber's, intentionally general, intended to highlight some of the religious differences among the broader traditions in Evangelicalism for sociological purposes. To the historians' certain dissatisfaction, I have not attempted to pursue the precise distinctions between myriad denominational traditions. It is my hope that this initial work will stimulate further typological refinements. For an elaboration of this argument, see J. D. Hunter, 1982. In terms of the denominational breakdown within these broader traditions, the following reference to this 1982 piece may be helpful: "Without claiming comprehensiveness, several of the major denominations which fit into the four religious traditions of Evangelicalism can be identified as follows: representative of denominations in the Baptist tradition are the Southern Baptist Convention of the U.S.A., the Disciples of Christ, many of the Churches of Christ, Plymouth Brethren, the Independent Fundamentalist Churches of America, the Independent Fundamentalist Bible Churches, the Seventh Day Adventists, the World Wide Church of God, and the Church of God International. In the Holiness-Pentecostal tradition, representative denominations are (Holiness) the Churches of God in North America, Church of God (Anderson, Ind.), the Wesleyan Church, the Church of the Nazarene, and the Church of Christ (Holiness) U.S.A., and (Pentecostal) the Church of God (Cleveland, Tenn.), the Church of God of Prophecy, the Full-Gospel Church Association, and the Assemblies of God. In the Reformed-Confessional tradition one may include such denominations as the Christian Reformed Church, the Orthodox Presbyterian Church, the Reformed Presbyterian Church-Evangelical Synod, the

Lutheran Church-Missouri Synod, the Evangelical Lutheran Synod, and the Association of Evangelical Lutheran Churches. Finally, denominations representative of the Anabaptist tradition are the Mennonite Church, General Conference Mennonite Church, Brethren in Christ Church, the Evangelical Mennonite Church, and the churches of the Evangelical Friends Alliance."

6. Kauffman and Harder (1975) provide the best social-scientific research on this subject to date.

Chapter 2

1. From the classical period in sociology, this has been a major theme. Beginning with Auguste Compte and the positivists there is the explicit contention that religion exists in a more primitive stage of human development, only to fade away with the evolutionary emergence of a scientific or positive stage. Durkheim (1965) also recognized the inevitable decline of traditional religion that accompanied the advancement and diffusion of science but felt confident that the old gods would be replaced by new gods of a different, secular sort. Weber (1964) as well foresaw the demise of religion in the modern gessellschaft; but unlike the others who viewed the displacement of religion as a positive replacement by a superior, more perfect culture, Weber regarded the displacement negatively. To him, an essentially rational and utilitarian culture represented an impoverishment: "With the progress of science and technology, man has stopped believing in magic powers, in spirits and demons; he has lost his sense of prophecy and, above all, his sense of the sacred. Reality has become dreary, flat and utilitarian, leaving a great void in the souls of men which they seek to fill by furious activity and through various devices and substitutes" (Fruend, 1968:24). This view has come down to the present; see P. Berger, 1969; Bibby, 1979; Wilson, 1966.

2. In Weber's opinion the extent of the rationalization process could be measured by the degree to which the mythical elements of thought are displaced by the trend toward systematic coherence (Gerth and Mills, 1946:51 f.).

3. This is one aspect of what Levy (1966:22ff.) refers to as the increasing gap in modern societies between myth and reality, between the real and the ideal.

4. Some relatively nonmodern cities (Corinth, Constantinople, Rome, etc.) evidenced undeniable signs of a cultural plurality, but this was the exception, not the rule. The difference between the relatively nonmodern and the relatively modern situations is quantitative. Sociocultural pluralism is a much more common feature of the latter.

5. In contrast, the relatively high degree of cultural integration in a relatively nonmodern situation means that a person's experience of the world and his perception of reality are also well integrated, unified, and virtually unshakable. People in this kind of setting share a world view within which all of the vagaries of human experience can be interpreted as implicitly "making sense." The same cultural symbols are operative in most situations for most people. The ordering impulse of reality definitions within such a world view is, of course with few exceptions, religious.

6. This is precisely the meaning of P. Berger's (1969:45) core sociology of knowledge concept, the *plausibility structure*.

7. Marx was first to stress this point; see Easton and Guddat, 1967:217–241.
8. Both the terms *cognitive bargaining* and *cognitive contamination* are borrowed from P. Berger.
9. Luckman, 1963, calls this accommodation "internal secularization."
10. Mandic (1970) presents a useful documentation of this in Eastern Europe, particularly in Yugoslavia; see also Bellah, 1976; J. D. Hunter, 1981.
11. This formulation offers one solution to that perplexing question of the future of religion in modern society—what is referred to in the sociology of religion as the secularization–persistence debate. Advocates of the secularization position (P. Berger, 1969; Martin, 1978; Swanson, 1968; Wilson, 1966; and the host of classical sociologists already mentioned) posit the nonlinear but inexorable demise of traditional forms of religion in the modern world. The advocates of the persistence position (Baum, 1970; Bell, 1977; Greeley, 1972; Parsons, 1963) contend that the former argument is unverifiable and that the religious needs of humankind have not changed noticeably with the advent of modernity. They cite statistics that point to the high degrees of religiosity among modern people. They maintain that religion abounds, in traditional and in new forms. My contention is that the secularization argument is only partially misguided in its prognosis. There appears to be little place for religious symbols in the daily activities of the public sphere. The public sphere continues to be dominated by functional rationality and, ipso facto, a highly secularized interpretation of reality; there is little if any evidence to the contrary. Where religion has survived and somtimes flourished is in the private sphere. Religion has not disappeared; it has only been relocated.
12. My position does not posit, according to Parsons, the necessity of a civil religion as a functional requirement for the maintenance of the social system; the opposite is more likely in most situations.
13. Compare the argument found in Fenn, 1978:chap. 4.
14. This is clear beginning with a reading of Bellah's 1967 article.

Chapter 3

1. On the predominance of this world view, cf. Handy, 1971:30 f.; Hudson, 1961: 109; Marsden, 1980:6, 11 ff.; Marty, 1970:144; McLoughlin, 1968:26. This was so despite denominational differences. Denominational factions had existed on a large scale since the Puritan immigrations of the early colonial period. There was, nonetheless, a widespread unity on central elements that cut across denominational loyalties.
2. The Baptists and Methodists and those denominations in the Baptist-Arminian tradition employed revivalistic techniques freely. Revivalism was found to a lesser extent in Congregationalism and Presbyterianism and to an even lesser extent in the Episcopal and Lutheran denominations.
3. For the single best history of the millenarian movement in the United States, see Sandeen, 1970b:94, 152, 163 f.
4. For a closer look at this view, see Abell, 1943. Also cf. Handy, 1971:159–170, 179 ff.; Marty, 1970:199–209.
5. This was for very clear sociologic reasons: the institutional pressures to ac-

count rationally for the supernatural in light of an increasingly popular and influential modern science, for example.

6. Indeed, the Fundamentalists supported the Baconian view of science. Anything not circumscribed by this paradigm was believed to be nonscientific.

7. The exceptions to this are the Northern European–immigrant, conservative denominations, Lutheran and Calvinist alike, which avoided much of this imbroglio.

8. Concerning this controversy, there are two excellent reviews: Furniss, 1954; Gatewood, 1969; cf. Marty, 1970:221–231; Sandeen, 1970b:246–269.

9. The variety of community studies that proliferated at this time document this fact. See Peterson and Demerath's review in their introduction to Pope, 1965:xxix f.

10. Pope (1965:86) documents this in his study of Gastonia, North Carolina.

11. On this point, see Pope, 1965:88. Illustrative is a portion of an interview Pope records: "In all my trials, Jesus is my refuge. I have been persecuted so much that I just smile now when someone persecutes me and cast it all on Jesus. I thank the Lord I am sanctified. I ain't never seen a talking picture show; people who goes to sech places cain't save nobody if they want to—you got to be different from the World. You got to live with Jesus! Me and Him lives alone and has a good time."

12. For a comprehensive review of the events that led up to the split in Fundamentalism and the establishment of the NAE, see Butler, 1977; Gaspar, 1963: 25–31.

13. On the new ecumenicism, see Marty, 1970:244–254; cf. H. Douglass, 1934.

14. For the alliance between conservative politics and Fundamentalism, see Clabaugh, 1974; Danzig, 1962; B. Johnson, 1962, 1964; Jorstad, 1970.

15. Data collected on the growth of the religious news media is reported in the *New York Times*, January 28, 1971:1.

16. The following is a partial list of concessions: A number of conciliatory positions were taken on the doctrine of creation. Typically the theory of seven 24-hour days was rejected in favor of variations whereby God personally intervened in the evolutionary process (e.g., the idea of "scientific creationism"). The doctrine of the inspiration of the Scriptures came to mean the guidance of those who were filled by the Holy Spirit as opposed to the theory that God dictated the Bible, word by word, to the biblical authors. Biblical hermeneutics came to mean the interpretation of the Bible literally, metaphorically, and so in, in terms of the intent of the writer, the textual context of the passage, and the historical setting of the writing as opposed to the crude literalism characteristic of Fundamentalism. Indeed, the inerrancy of the Scriptures acquired the meaning that the Bible, though the Word of God and unmistaken in its statements and teachings, could, nonetheless, contain minor technical mistakes such as a miscalculated genealogy.

17. Though the Fundamentalism of the 1920s, 1930s, and 1940s barely resembles what exists today except in core doctrinal features, pockets of a militant separatism may still be found. The legacy of Bob Jones and Bob Jones University is notable in this regard. The quarrels between Bob Jones III and Jerry Falwell in 1980, as recorded in Falwell's *Moral Majority Report*, are reminis-

cent—mostly in spirit, not in substantive details—of the quarrels between Fundamentalists and neo-Evangelicals in the 1950s and early 1960s. Thus the term *Fundamentalism*, as descriptive of conservative Protestantism toward the end of the twentieth century, still has some, though qualified, utility.

Chapter 4

1. Cf. Perry's (1959) qualitative analysis of American Fundamentalism and social class.
2. The data presented here is reconfirmed in other surveys, most notably Gallup, 1978.

Chapter 5

1. A distinction between the concepts *biblical inerrancy* and *biblical infallibility* is made by theological elites but not by the laity as a whole; I therefore do not make the distinction here. See Lindsell, 1976, p. 27 n. 1.
2. The extent of this trust is illustrated by Lindsell in his controversial *Battle for the Bible* (1976), a book written for laymen: "Whatever it [the Bible] communicates is to be trusted and can be relied upon as being true. The Bible is not a textbook on chemistry, astronomy, philosophy or medicine. But when it speaks on matters having to do with these or any other subjects, the Bible does not lie to us" (p. 18).

Chapter 6

1. Bright takes these types from the nineteenth-century Keswick teachings; cf. Marsden, 1980:248 n. 24.
2. The Gallup/Christianity Today data (J. D. Hunter, 1980b) show that 28.8 percent of all Evangelicals identify themselves as "charismatic Christians." Of those identifying themselves in this way, 34.7 percent claim to have spoken in tongues. See Quebedeaux (1976) for a closer look at this phenomenon.
3. In a real-life demonstration of this irony, *Newsweek*, November 10, 1980, recorded a widely publicized example of a slip of incivility: "At the meeting [the National Affairs Briefing for Evangelical leaders], Rev. Bailey Smith, the fundamentalist president of the Southern Baptist Convention declared: 'It is interesting at great political rallies how you have a Protestant to pray and a Catholic to pray, and then you have a Jew to pray. With all due respect to these dear people, my friends, God Almighty does not hear the prayer of a Jew.'"
4. A slightly modified version of this appeared as J. D. Hunter, "Subjectivization and the New Evangelical Theodicy," *Journal for the Scientific Study of Religion* 20(1982):39–47.
5. Institutional accommodation may be seen in churches' establishment of church and parachurch counseling services and in their frequent requirement that ministers have professional training in counseling.

Chapter 7

1. For a broader review of the issues than is required here, see Falwell, 1980b and Rowe, 1976.
2. In conventional political activity, the New Class tends to support candidates who endorse these values and positions. In the past decades, presidential candidates they have supported include Adlai Stevenson, George McGovern, Jimmy Carter, and John Anderson.
3. Rowe, 1976, elaborates on many of these strategies.
4. In the larger and more significant struggle between an older business class and the new knowledge class, one could speculate on the role of the Evangelical political movement. Optimists such as Rifkin (1979) have argued that politicized Evangelicals may go through the necessary changes to assert themselves as a bold and independent political force capable of rallying large numbers of people and wielding a measure of political power in new and creative directions. There may, on the other hand, be a serious backlash within the Evangelical community, which could neutralize any initiatives spawned by the religious New Right. There may also be a continued alliance with the older business class in accomplishing the conservative political agenda. Such an alliance may continue until the Evangelicals' agenda has been set in motion or until they embarrass themselves out of an alliance. (Senator Barry Goldwater's repudiation of the Moral Majority might be seen in this context.) In either case, Evangelical political sentiments may prove, in the last analysis, to be manipulated as a strategic device of the older business class.
5. Evangelicals parallel non-Evangelicals on this general continuum (Gallup, 1980b).
6. An alternative interpretation of Evangelical political activism comes from a history-of-religion perspective which argues that every significant revival of conservative Protestant religion (the First and Second Great Awakenings most notably) was followed by a turn toward social and political activism. Thus what we see in the early 1980s is merely a response to the so-called Third Great Awakening, the Evangelical revival of the 1970s, and modernity has nothing to do with it. In response, one could first question whether a revival did in fact occur in the 1970s or whether what was touted as revival was merely a media event. Second, if one agrees that there was a revival, what was its cause? Did it occur outside of the influence of social factors or possibly as a partial reaction to modern social and cultural change? If one considers the latter possible, then this history-of-religion interpretation does not necessarily preclude my interpretation.

Chapter 8

1. Granting credence to the Evangelical's belief that the God of the Judeo-Christian heritage has an ontological status apart from human affairs does not preclude the role of projection in the culture. By entering into the course of human history (in acts of revelation), he would necessarily subject himself to the (undoubtedly humiliating) process of enculturation. His image would become re-

constituted through these processes in terms comprehensible to the people of a particular society in a particular period in its history.

2. The "testimonies" of Tam (1969) and LeTourneau (1967) provide two accounts of this practice; see also Herron's *A Christian Executive in a Secular World* (1979).

Chapter 9

1. Here I refer to Rifkin's *The Emerging Order* (1979). Rifkin posits a very interesting thesis in the notion of a "Second Reformation" or Third Great Awakening based on a new covenant of economic and ecological conservation. In light of the data presented here, Rifkin's thesis looks like wishful thinking. He argues that the basis of a future ethic of conservation in the coming years of economic scarcity lies in the Evangelical-charismatic movement, yet he presumes that contemporary Evangelicals and charismatics maintain the same attitude of moral and vocational asceticism as their eighteenth- and nineteenth-century counterparts. In fact, he builds much of his argument on a review of pretwentieth-century Protestant experience. The little evidence he derives from the contemporary scene comes from the ideas of a few Evangelical intellectuals (Francis Schaeffer in particular) and not from empirical data on the mainstream. Research on contemporary mainstream Evangelicalism does not provide sufficient evidence to warrant this optimistic projection.

Bibliography

Evangelical sources are in a separate section that follows the scholarly sources.

Scholarly Sources

Abell, Aaron
  1943   *The urban impact on American protestantism, 1865–1900.* Cambridge: Cambridge University Press.
Acquaviva, A.
  1960   The psychology of de-Christianization. *Social Compass* 7:209–225.
Ahlstrom, Sydney
  1972   *A religious history of the American people.* New Haven: Yale University Press.
Allport, Gordon
  1950   *The individual and his religion.* New York: Macmillan.
American Civil Liberties Union
  1980   If the Moral Majority has its way, you'd better start praying. *New York Times,* November 23. (Advertisement)
Aron, Raymond
  1970   *Main currents in sociological thought.* Vol. 2. New York: Doubleday.
Ballard, Paul
  1976   Evangelical experience: Notes on the history of a tradition. *Journal of Ecumenical Studies* 13(1):51–68.
Barr, James
  1977   *Fundamentalism.* London: Student Christian Movement.
Baum, Gregory
  1970   Does the world remain disenchanted? *Social Research* 37(2):153–202.
Bell, Daniel
  1964   *The radical right.* New York: Doubleday.
  1971   Religion in the sixties. *Social Research* 38(3):447–497.
  1976   *The cultural contradictions of capitalism.* New York: Basic Books.
  1977   The return of the sacred. *British Journal of Sociology* 28(4):419–450.

Bellah, R.
    1967   Civil religion in America. *Daedelus* 96(1):1–21.
    1976   New religious consciousness and the crisis of modernity. In *The new religious consciousness*, ed. C. Glock and R. Bellah, chap. 16. Berkeley and Los Angeles: University of California Press.
Berger, Brigitte
    1971   *Societies in change.* New York: Basic Books.
Berger, Peter L.
    1961   *The noise of solemn assemblies.* New York: Doubleday.
    1963   A market model for the analysis of ecumenicity. *Social Research* 30(1): 77–93.
    1969   *The sacred canopy.* New York: Doubleday.
    1970   *A rumor of angels.* New York: Doubleday.
    1975   Religion. *Fortune,* April, pp. 134–138.
    1976   Modern identity: Crisis and continuity. In *The cultural drama,* ed. Wilton Dillon. Washington: Smithsonian.
    1978a Ethics and the New Class. *Worldview,* April, pp. 6–11.
    1978b *Facing up to modernity.* New York: Basic Books.
    1979   *The heretical imperative.* New York: Doubleday.
Berger, Peter L.; Berger, Brigitte; and Kellner, Hansfried
    1974   *The homeless mind.* New York: Doubleday.
Berger, Peter L.; and Luckmann, Thomas
    1966a Secularization and pluralism. *Yearbook for the Sociology of Religion* 2:73–90.
    1966b *The social construction of reality.* New York: Doubleday.
Berger, P.; and Neuhaus, R., eds.
    1976   *Against the world for the world.* New York: Seabury.
Bibby, R.
    1979   Religion and modernity: The Canadian case. *Journal for the Scientific Study of Religion* 19:1–17.
Bibby, R.; and Brinkerhoff, M.
    1973   The circulation of the saints: A study of people who join conservative churches. *Journal for the Scientific Study of Religion* 12:273–282.
Bloesch, Donald
    1973   *The Evangelical renaissance.* Grand Rapids: Eerdmans.
Bodenheimer, S.
    1968   The ideology of developmentalism. *Berkeley Journal of Sociology* 35: 130–159.
Boulding, Kenneth
    1964   *The meaning of the twentieth century.* New York: Harper & Row.
Brode, J., ed.
    1969   *The process of modernization: An annotated bibliography.* Cambridge, Mass.: Harvard University Press.
Bruce-Briggs, B.
    1979   *The New Class?* New Brunswick, N.J.: Transaction.

Butler, Farley
   1977   Billy Graham and the end of Evangelical unity. *Dissertation Abstracts International* 37:4429A–4430A.
Caporale, R.; and Grumelli, A.
   1971   *The culture of unbelief.* Berkeley and Los Angeles: University of California Press.
Cavert, Samuel
   1968   *The American churches in the ecumenical movement, 1900–1968.* New York: Association Press.
Chartier, M.; and Goehner, Larry
   1976   A study of the relationship of parent–adolescent communication, self-esteem, and God image. *Journal of Psychology and Theology* 4(3):277–282.
Clabaugh, Gary
   1974   *Thunder on the right.* Chicago: Nelson-Hall.
Crawford, Alan
   1980   *Thunder on the right.* New York: Pantheon.
Cuddihy, John
   1974   *Sigmund Freud's ordeal of civility.* Ph.D. dissertation, Rutgers University.
   1978   *No offense: Civil religion and Protestant taste.* New York: Seabury.
Danzig, David
   1962   The radical right and the rise of the Fundamentalist majority. *Commentary* 33(4):291–298.
Dayton, Donald
   1976   *Discovering an Evangelical heritage.* New York: Harper & Row.
   1980   *Millennial views and social reform in nineteenth century America.* Unpublished manuscript, Northern Baptist Theological Seminary.
Dejong, G. F.; and Ford, T. R.
   1965   Religious Fundamentalism and denominational preference in the southern Appalachian region. *Journal for the Scientific Study of Religion* 5:24–33.
Douglass, H. Paul
   1934   *Church unity movements in the United States.* New York: Institute of Social and Religious Research.
Douglass, M.
   1973   *Natural symbols.* New York: Random House, Vintage.
Durkheim, Emile
   1964   *The division of labor in society.* New York: Free Press.
   1965   *The elementary forms of the religious life.* New York: Free Press.
Dynes, R.
   1955   Church–sect typology and socio-economic status. *American Journal of Sociology* 20:555–560.
Easton, L.; and Guddat, K., eds.
   1967   *The writings of young Marx.* New York: Doubleday.
Eisenstadt, S.
   1966   *Modernization.* Englewood Cliffs, N.J.: Prentice-Hall.

1968   *The Protestant ethic and modernization.* New York: Basic Books.

1973   *Tradition, change, and modernization.* New York: Wiley.

Elinson, Howard

1965   The implications of Pentecostal religion for intellectualism, politics and race relations. *American Journal of Sociology* 70:403–415.

Ellul, Jacques

1964   *The technological society.* New York: Random House, Vintage.

Ethridge, F. M.; and Feagin, J. R.

1979   Varieties of "Fundamentalism": A conceptual and empirical analysis of two Protestant denominations. *Sociological Quarterly* 20:37–48.

Falding, Harold

1977   Made in the likeness of God. *Sociological Analysis* 40:147–157.

Feagin, J. R.

1964   Prejudice and religious types: A focused study of southern Fundamentalists. *Journal for the Scientific Study of Religion* 4:3–13.

Fenn, Richard

1969   The secularization of values. *Journal for the Scientific Study of Religion* 8:112–124.

1970   The process of secularization: A post Parsonian view. *Journal for the Scientific Study of Religion* 9:117–136.

1972   Toward a new sociology of religion. *Journal for the Scientific Study of Religion* 11:16–32.

1974   Religion and the legitimation of social systems. In *Changing perspectives in the scientific study of religion,* ed. Allan Eister, pp. 143–162. New York: Wiley.

1978   *Toward a theory of secularization.* Storrs, Conn.: Society for the Scientific Study of Religion.

Feuerback, Ludwig

1957   *The essence of christianity.* New York: Harper & Row.

Freud, Sigmund

1953   *The future of an illusion.* New York: Liveright.

Fruend, Julien

1968   *The sociology of Max Weber.* New York: Pantheon.

Furniss, Normon

1954   *The Fundamentalist controversy, 1918–1931.* New Haven: Yale University Press.

Gallup, G.

1978   *The unchurched Americans study.* Princeton: Princeton Religious Research Center.

1980a Evangelical Christianity in the United States. Princeton: Princeton Religious Research Center.

1980b The political impact of Evangelicals. Pt. 1. News release from the Gallup Poll.

1980c The political impact of Evangelicals. Pt. 2. News release from the Gallup Poll.

Gaspar, Louis

1963   *The Fundamentalist movement.* Paris: Mouton.

Gatewood, Willard
    1969 *Controversy in the twenties: Fundamentalism, modernism, and evolu-
          tion.* Nashville: Vanderbilt University Press.
Gehlen, A.
    1957 *Die Seele im technischen Zeitalte.* Hamburg: Rowohlt.
    1980 *Man in the age of technology.* Oxford: Oxford University Press.
Gerth, H.; and Mills, C.
    1946 *On Max Weber.* New York: Oxford University Press.
Glennon, L.
    1979 *Women and dualism.* New York: Longman.
Glock, C.; Ringer, B.; and Babbie, E.
    1967 *To comfort and to challenge.* Berkeley and Los Angeles: University of
          California Press.
Glock, C.; and Stark, R.
    1965 *Religion and society in tension.* Skokie, Ill.: Rand McNally.
Goldsen, Rose; Rosenberg, Morris; Williams, Robin; and Suchman, Edward
    1960 *What college students think.* New York: Van Nostrand.
Gorsuch, R.; and McFarland, S.
    1972 Single vs. multiple-item scales for measuring religious values. *Journal
          for the Scientific Study of Religion* 11:53–65.
Gouldner, Alvin
    1978 The New Class project 1 and 2. *Theory and Society*, Fall.
Grafton, T. H.
    1941 Religious origins and sociological theory. *American Sociological Review*
          10:726–739.
Greeley, A.
    1972 *Unsecular man.* New York: Dell.
    1974 Religion in a secular society. *Social Research* 44(2):206–240.
Greven, Philip
    1977 *The Protestant temperament.* New York: Knopf.
Grupp, F. W.; and Newman, W.
    1973 Political ideology and religious preference: The John Birch Society
          and the Americans for Democratic Action. *Journal for the Scientific
          Study of Religion* 12:401–413.
Gusfield, J.
    1963 *Symbolic crusade: Status politics and the American temperance move-
          ment.* Urbana: University of Illinois Press.
Habermas, J.
    1974 The public sphere. *New German Critique* 3:49–55.
Hadden, J.
    1969 *The gathering storm in the churches.* New York: Doubleday.
Hammond, J.
    1979 *The politics of benevolence.* Norwood, N.J.: Ablex.
Hammond, P.
    1974 Religious pluralism and Durkheim's integration thesis. In *Changing
          perspectives in the scientific study of religion*, ed. Allan Eister, pp.
          115–142. New York: Wiley.

Handy, Robert
    1971   A Christian America. New York: Oxford University Press.
Heilman, S.
    1978   Constructing orthodoxy. Society 15(4):32–40.
Herberg, Will
    1955   Protestant Catholic Jew. New York: Doubleday, Anchor.
Holzner, Burkart
    1968   Reality construction in society. Cambridge, Mass.: Schenkman.
Horowitz, Irving
    1979   On the expansion of new theories and the withering away of old
           classes. Society 16(2):55–62.
Hudson, Willard
    1961   Protestant America. Chicago: University of Chicago Press.
Hunter, J. D.
    1980a Analysis of the Gallup/Christianity Today data. Unpublished manu-
           script.
    1980b The Young Evangelicals and the New Class. Review of Religious Re-
           search 22(2):155–169.
    1981   The new religions: Demodernization and the protest against modernity.
           In The new religions, ed. Bryan R. Wilson. New York: Rose of Sharon.
    1982   Operationalizing Evangelicalism: A review, critique, and proposal.
           Sociological Analysis 42:363–372.
    1983   The liberal reaction to the new Christian right. In The new Christian
           right, ed. Robert Liebman and Robert Wuthnow. Chicago: Aldine.
Johnson, B.
    1962   Ascetic Protestantism and political preference. Public Opinion Quarterly
           2:35–46.
    1964   Ascetic Protestantism and political preference in the Deep South. Amer-
           ican Journal of Sociology 69:356–366.
Johnson, Jon
    1980   Will Evangelicalism survive its own popularity? Grand Rapids: Zon-
           dervan.
Jones, Charles
    1974   Perfectionist persuasion: The Holiness movement and American Meth-
           odism, 1867–1936. Metuchen, N.J.: Scarecrow.
Jorstad, Erling
    1970   The politics of doomsday. Nashville: Abingdon.
Kahl, J.
    1959   Some social concomitants of industrialization and urbanization. Hu-
           man Organization 18(2):53–74.
Kauffman, J. Howard; and Harder, Leland
    1975   Anabaptists four centuries later. Scottsdale, Penn.: Herald.
Kelsey, George
    1973   Social ethics among Southern Baptists. Metuchen, N.J.: Scarecrow.
Keyser, M.; and Collins, G.
    1976   Parental image and the concept of God. Journal of Psychology and
           Theology 4(1):68–80.

Kristol, Irving
    1978   *Two cheers for capitalism*. New York: Basic Books.
Lasch, C.
    1978   *The culture of narcissism*. New York: Norton.
Levy, M.
    1966   *Modernization and the structure of societies*. Princeton: Princeton University Press.
    1972   *Modernization: Latecomers and survivors*. New York: Basic Books.
Lippmann, W.
    1929   *A preface to morals*. New York: Macmillan.
Lipset, S. M.
    1963   *The first new nation*. New York: Doubleday.
Lipset, S. M.; and Raab, Earl
    1970   *The politics of unreason*. New York: Harper & Row.
Luckmann, Thomas
    1963   On religion and modern society. *Journal for the Scientific Study of Religion* 2:53–74.
    1967   *The invisible religion*. New York: Macmillan.
Lynd, R. S.; and Lynd, H. M.
    1929   *Middletown*. New York: Harcourt, Brace.
    1937   *Middletown in transition*. New York: Harcourt, Brace.
Machlup, Fritz
    1962   *The production and distribution of knowledge in the United States*. Princeton: Princeton University Press.
Mandic, Oleg
    1970   A Marxist perspective on contemporary religious revivals. *Social Research* 37(2):237–258.
Maranell, G.
    1974   *Responses to religion: Studies in social psychology of religious belief*. Lawrence: University of Kansas Press.
Marcuse, H.
    1964   *One dimensional man*. Boston: Beacon.
Marsden, George
    1980   *Fundamentalism and American culture*. New York: Oxford University Press.
Martin, David
    1978   *A general theory of secularization*. New York: Harper & Row.
Marty, Martin
    1970   *Righteous empire*. New York: Dial.
    1976   *A nation of behaviors*. Chicago: University of Chicago Press.
McFaul, Thomas
    1973   Which way the future? *Journal for the Scientific Study of Religion* 12:231–236.
McLoughlin, William G.
    1955   *Billy Sunday was his real name*. Chicago: University of Chicago Press.
    1959   *Modern revivalism: Charles Grandison Finney to Billy Graham*. New York: Ronald.
    1968   *The American Evangelicals, 1800–1900*. New York: Harper & Row.

McNamara, P.

1973   Comment on Fenn's "Toward a new sociology of religion." *Journal for the Scientific Study of Religion* 12:237–239.

Moberg, D.

1972   *The great reversal: Evangelism and social concern.* Philadelphia: Lippincott.

Morgan, Edmund

1966   *The Puritan family.* New York: Harper & Row.

Murch, James

1952   *The growing super-church.* Cinncinatti: National Association of Evangelicals.

Nisbet, R.

1955   *The quest for community.* New York: Oxford University Press.

Orum, A. M.

1970   Religion and the rise of the radical white: The case of southern Wallace support in 1968. *Social Science Quarterly* 50:674–688.

Outler, Albert, ed.

1964   *John Wesley.* New York: Oxford University Press.

Parsons, T.

1963   Christianity and modern industrial society. In *Sociological theory, values and socio-cultural change*, ed. E. Tiryakian, pp. 33–70. New York: Free Press.

1966   *Societies: Evolutionary and comparative perspectives.* Englewood Cliffs, N.J.: Prentice-Hall.

1969   On the concept of value commitment. *Sociological Inquiry* 38(3):135–160.

Perry, Everett

1959   *Socio-economic factors and American Fundamentalism.* Ph.D. dissertation, University of Chicago.

Polanyi, Karl

1944   *The great transformation.* Boston: Beacon.

Pope, Liston

1965   *Millhands and preachers.* New Haven: Yale University Press.

Quebedeaux, Richard

1974   *The Young Evangelicals.* New York: Harper & Row.

1976   *The new charismatics.* New York: Doubleday.

1978   *The worldly Evangelicals.* New York: Harper & Row.

Redfield, R.

1940   The folk society and culture. *American Journal of Sociology* 45:731–742.

1947   The folk society. *American Journal of Sociology* 52:293–308.

Rifkin, Jeremy

1979   *The emerging order.* New York: Putnam's.

Robertson, R.

1974   Religious and sociological factors in the analysis of secularization. In *Changing perspectives in the scientific study of religion*, ed. Allan Eister, pp. 41–60. New York: Wiley.

Roof, W. C.
  1976 Traditional religion in contemporary society: A theory of local–cosmopolitan plausibility. *American Sociological Review* 41:195–208.
  1978 *Community and commitment: Religious plausibility in a liberal Protestant church.* New York: Elsevier-North Holland.

Rudnick, Milton
  1966 *Fundamentalism and the Missouri Synod.* St. Louis: Concordia.

Sandeen, Ernest
  1968 *The origins of Fundamentalism.* New York: Fawcett.
  1970a Fundamentalism and American identity. *Annals of the American Academy of Politics and Social Science* 38:56–65.
  1970b *The roots of Fundamentalism.* Chicago: Chicago University Press.

Schlesinger, Arthur; and Fox, Dixon Ryan, eds.
  1933 *A history of American life, 1878–1898.* New York: Macmillan.

Schutz, Alfred
  1970 *On phenomenology and social relations.* Edited by Helmut Wagner. Chicago: University of Chicago Press.
  1976 *Collected papers.* Vol. 2. The Hague: Martinus Nijhoff.

Schweitzer, Albert
  1948 *The quest for the historic Jesus.* New York: Macmillan.

Sennett, R.
  1978 *The fall of public man.* New York: Random House, Vintage.

Shiner, L.
  1967 The concept of secularization in empirical research. *Journal for the Scientific Study of Religion* 6:207–220.

Shupe, Anson; and Stacey, William
  1983 *An assessment of grass-roots support for the new religious right.* In *The new Christian right,* ed. Robert Liebman and Robert Wuthnow. Chicago: Aldine.

Simmel, Georg
  1900 *The philosophy of money.* Munich and Leipzig: Duncker and Humblot.

Simpson, John
  1983 Support for the Moral Majority and status politics in contemporary America. In *The new Christian right,* ed. Robert Liebman and Robert Wuthnow. Chicago: Aldine.

Smart, Ninian
  1973 *The science of religion and the sociology of knowledge.* Princeton: Princeton University Press.

Smith, Timothy
  1976 *Revivalism and social reform: American Protestantism on the eve of the Civil War.* Gloucester, Mass.: Peter Smith.

Stark, R.; and Glock, C.
  1968 *American piety: The nature of religious commitment.* Berkeley and Los Angeles: University of California Press.

Stauffer, R.
  1974 Civil religion, technocracy and the private sphere. *Journal for the Scientific Study of Religion* 13:415–425.

Stellway, R. J.
  1973 The correspondence between religious orientation and socio-political liberalism and conservativism. *Sociological Quarterly* 14:430–439.
Streiker, Lowell; and Strober, Gerald
  1972 *Religion and the new majority.* New York: Association Press.
Swanson, Guy
  1968 Modern secularity: Its meaning, sources and interpretation. In *The religious situation,* ed. D. Cutler, pp. 801–834. Boston: Beacon.
Teggart, F.
  1918 *The process of history.* New Haven: Yale University Press.
Tonnies, F.
  1957 *Community and society.* New York: Harper & Row.
Turner, Ralph
  1976 The real self: From institution to impulse. *American Journal of Sociology* 81:989–1016.
Warner, R. S.
  1979 Theoretical barriers to the understanding of Evangelical Christianity. *Sociological Analysis* 40:1–9.
Weber, Max
  1958 *The Protestant ethic and the spirit of capitalism.* New York: Scribner's.
  1964 *The sociology of religion.* Boston: Beacon.
Wells, D.; and Woodridge, J., eds.
  1975 *The Evangelicals.* Nashville: Abingdon.
Wierd, Barbara
  1973 *From separatism to evangelism: A case study, 1940–1970.* Ph.D. dissertation, University of Pennsylvania.
Wilson, Brian
  1966 *Religion in a secular society.* London: C. A. Watts.
  1976 *Contemporary transformations of religion.* Oxford: Oxford University Press.
Wolff, Kurt
  1964 *The sociology of Georg Simmel.* New York: Free Press.
Wuthnow, R.
  1976a *The consciousness reformation.* Berkeley and Los Angeles: University of California Press.
  1976b Recent patterns of secularization: A problem of generations. *American Sociological Review* 41:850–867.
  1978 *Experimentation and American religion.* Berkeley and Los Angeles: University of California Press.
  1983 The political rebirth of American Evangelicalism. In *The new Christian right,* ed. Robert Liebman and Robert Wuthnow. Chicago: Aldine.
Yankelovich, Daniel
  1981 *New rules in American life.* New York: Random.
Yinger, Milton
  1967 Pluralism, religion, and secularism. *Journal for the Scientific Study of Religion* 6:17–30.

Yoder, John H.
1972 *The politics of Jesus.* Grand Rapids: Eerdmans.
Zijderveld, A.
1970 *The abstract society.* New York: Doubleday.
1972 The anti-institutional mood. *Worldview* 15(9):32–36.

Evangelical Sources

Adolph, Paul E.
1956 *Release from tension.* Chicago: Moody.
Ahlem, Lloyd H.
1973 *Do I have to be me?* Glendale, Calif.: Regal.
1978 *How to cope with conflict, crisis, and change.* Glendale, Calif.: Regal.
Allen, Charles
1953 *God's psychiatry.* Old Tappan, N.J.: Revell.
1968 *Roads to radiant living.* Old Tappan, N.J.: Revell.
Augsburger, David
1970 *Be all you can be.* Carol Stream, Ill.: Creation House.
Bakker, Jim
1977 *The big three mountain-movers.* Plainfield, N.J.: Logos International.
Billings, William
1980a *The Christian's political action manual.* Washington, D.C.: National Christian Action Coalition.
1980b *What it means to be "pro-family."* Washington, D.C.: National Christian Action Coalition.
Blanchard, John
1978 *Right with God.* Chicago: Moody.
Brandt, Henry
1978 *I want happiness now!* Grand Rapids: Zondervan.
Bright, Bill
1965 *Four spiritual laws.* San Bernardino, Calif.: Campus Crusade for Christ.
1971 *The transferable concepts series.* Nos. 1–9. San Bernardino, Calif.: Campus Crusade for Christ.
1976 *Your five duties as a Christian citizen.* San Bernardino, Calif.: Campus Crusade for Christ.
Bustanby, Andre
1977 *You can change your personality.* Grand Rapids: Zondervan.
Caldwell, Louis
1978 *You can prevent a nervous breakdown.* Grand Rapids: Baker Book House.
Carlson, Dwight
1976 *Living God's will.* Old Tappan, N.J.: Revell.
Collins, Gary
1969 *Search for reality.* Santa Ana, Calif.: Vision House.
1977 *Relax and live longer.* Santa Ana, Calif.: Vision House.

Conway, Sally
    1980 *You and your husband's mid-life crisis.* Elgin, Ill.: Cook.
Cook, Robert
    1978a *Now that I believe.* Chicago: Moody.
    1978b *Walk with the King today.* Chappaqua, N.Y.: Christian Herald.
Cosgrove, Mark P.; and Mallory, James D.
    1977 *Mental health: A Christian approach.* Grand Rapids: Zondervan.
Cramer, Raymond
    1980 *Psychology of Jesus and mental health.* Grand Rapids: Zondervan.
Dugan, LeRoy
    1973 *How to live the Jesus life.* Minneapolis: Bethany Fellowship.
Eggum, Tom
    1979 *Feeling good about feeling bad.* Nashville: Nelson.
Falwell, Jerry
    1980a *Letter of appeal.* Moral Majority, August 14.
    1980b *Listen America!* New York: Doubleday.
Falwell, Jerry, ed.
    1981 *How you can help clean up America.* Washington, D.C.: Moral
        Majority.
Flynn, Leslie
    1980 *The gift of joy.* Wheaton, Ill.: Scripture.
Foster, Robert
    n.d.   *Seven minutes with God.* Colorado Springs: Navpress.
Foster, Timothy
    1980 *You and God.* Wheaton, Ill.: Victor.
Graham, Billy
    1977 *How to be born again.* Waco, Tex.: Word.
Grimes, Howard
    1979 *How to become your own best self.* Waco, Tex.: Word.
Haggai, John
    1967 *How to win over worry.* Grand Rapids: Zondervan.
Helms, Jesse
    1976 *When free men shall stand.* Grand Rapids: Zondervan.
Herron, Orley
    1979 *A Christian executive in a secular world.* Nashville: Nelson.
Hubbard, David
    1976 *Happiness: You can find the secret.* Wheaton, Ill.: Tyndale House.
Hunter, John
    1972 *World in rebellion.* Chicago: Moody.
Josephson, Elmer
    1976 *God's key to health and happiness.* Old Tappan, N.J.: Revell.
Kennedy, D. James
    1977 *Evangelism explosion.* Wheaton, Ill.: Tyndale House.
Kilgore, James
    1977 *Being up in a down world.* Irvine, Calif.: Harvest House.
Kroll, W.
    1980 Sexual patterns degenerating. *Moral Majority Report* 1:11–16.

LaHaye, Tim
1974 *How to win over depression.* Grand Rapids: Zondervan.
1980 *Battle for the mind.* Old Tappan, N.J.: Revell.
1981 *Transformed temperaments.* Wheaton, Ill.: Tyndale House.
Larson, Bruce
1972 *Dare to live now.* Grand Rapids: Zondervan.
LeTourneau, R. G.
1967 *Mover of men and mountains.* Chicago: Moody.
Lindsell, H.
1976 *Battle for the Bible.* Grand Rapids: Zondervan.
Lutzer, Erwin
1974 *How in this world can I be holy?* Chicago: Moody.
McAteer, Edward
1980 *Is there not a cause?* Arlington, Va.: Roundtable.
Narramore, Clyde
1969 *This way to happiness.* Grand Rapids: Zondervan.
Narramore, Clyde; and Narramore, Ruth
1975 *How to handle pressure.* Wheaton, Ill.: Tyndale House.
Nelson, Marion
1974 *Why Christians crack up.* Chicago: Moody.
Nieboer, Joe
1953 *How to be a happy Christian.* Neptune, N.J.: Loizeaux.
Noorbergen, Rene; and Hood, Ralph
1980 *The death cry of an eagle.* Grand Rapids: Zondervan.
Nordtvedt, Matilda
1976 *Defeating despair and depression.* Chicago: Moody.
Osborne, Cecil
1968 *The art of understanding yourself.* Grand Rapids: Zondervan.
1980 *The art of getting along with people.* Grand Rapids: Zondervan.
Pippert, Rebecca
1979 *Out of the salt shaker and into the world.* Downers Grove, Ill.: Inter-
Varsity.
Price, John
1976 *America at the crossroads.* Wheaton, Ill.: Tyndale House.
Richards, Larry
1977 *Born to grow.* Wheaton, Ill.: Scripture.
Roberts, Oral
1978 *How to get through your struggles.* Old Tappan, N.J.: Revell.
Rowe, H. Edward
1976 *Save America.* Old Tappan, N.J.: Revell, Spire.
1980 *Deciding how to vote.* Arlington, Va.: Roundtable.
Sall, Millard
1977 *Faith, psychology and Christian maturity.* Grand Rapids: Zondervan.
Schmidt, Jerry
1978 *You can help youself.* Irvine, Calif.: Harvest House.
Schuller, Robert
1969 *Self-love.* Old Tappan, N.J.: Revell, Spire.

1973   *You can become the person you want to be.* Old Tappan, N.J.: Revell, Spire.

1979   *Move ahead with possibility thinking.* Old Tappan, N.J.: Revell.

Seymour, Richard

1977   *Religion: Who needs it?* Chicago: Moody.

Sisson, Richard

1979   *Training for evangelism.* Chicago: Moody.

Stanford, Miles

1976   *Principles of spiritual growth.* Lincoln, Neb.: Back to the Bible.

Sumrall, Lester

1979   *Living free.* Nashville: Scepter.

Sweeting, George

1974   *Is America dying?* Chicago: Moody.

1976a *How to begin the Christian life.* Chicago: Moody.

1976b A *National Call to Renewal.* Chicago: Moody.

Tam, Stanley

1969   *God owns my business.* Waco, Tex.: Word.

Wagner, Maurice

1979   *The sensation of being somebody: Building an adequate self concept.* Grand Rapids: Zondervan.

Walton, Rus

1975   *One nation under God.* Old Tappan, N.J.: Revell.

Index